PURIM

OR

THE FEAST OF ESTHER

An Historical Study

BY

N. S. DONIACH

Sometime Hody Scholar of Wadham College, Oxford.

PHILADELPHIA
THE JEWISH PUBLICATION SOCIETY OF AMERICA
1933

PRINTED AT
THE JEWISH PUBLICATION SOCIETY PRESS
PHILADELPHIA, PENNA.

To My Mother

"On dit même que les juifs, encore aujourd'hui, célèbrent par de grandes actions de grâces le jour où leurs ancêtres furent délivrés par Esther de la cruauté d'Aman."

(Racine, Preface to *Esther*).

CONTENTS

PREFACE

No one will be more keenly conscious than I am of the imperfectness of this attempt not only to describe Purim but also to solve the problems of its origin and history. Rather than give reasons for the inconsistencies which may be found in this book, I would crave the reader's indulgence on the plea that, to the best of my knowledge, this is the first attempt to give so detailed a portrayal of a Jewish festival. It is to the credit of the Jewish Publication Society of America that, appreciating this, they took up the book in spite of its faults. In thanking them I should like also to thank those of my friends who helped and encouraged me and to mention by name L. G. Bishop, I. Berlin and S. Golt, the last mentioned having compiled the index.

London, 1933

INTRODUCTION

THERE is a genius for festivals in Jewry —a genius which speaks eloquently of the antiquity of Israel's traditions. Primitive man in surrendering his portable tent of camel's hair for the mud cabin, and in leaving his search after new pastures to plant fields with corn, was sensible of a new divinity which shaped his fortunes. No longer did the tree, the bush by night, the fantastic stone, the sudden lightning and all the whimsicalities of Pan inspire his only reverence. It was no longer an animistic world which ruled him. Rather was it the sun and moon in their set courses, the seasonal rains and an ordered and fertile nature which held him in their thrall.

The round of Israel's festivals was at first nothing more than a cycle of agricultural celebrations. They mark the change of mind in Abraham's descendants when, beginning to till the fertile valleys of Canaan, they ascribed new attributes to the God of Moses. Forthwith they sought to placate a stern nature and to give honor to her fruitfulness. But Purim is a festival of different origin; it commemorates one particular Jewish victory. It is preeminently the festival of the light heart—a time of jesting and of fooling, not unlike the Venetian celebrations of King Carnival, or the rites of the Lord of Misrule in medieval France.

Whether there are indications in the book of Esther of the previous observance of a similar festival outside Israel, is a question which we shall later be obliged to discuss. Lest we may appear, however, to lose sight of the artistry and the beauty of this book, it may be well to accord it in this place a tribute. It is a simple story, a perennial spring that feeds the river of Jewish fairy tales. Queen Scheherazade may perhaps be some pale reflection of our heroine. But it is more than a story, more than a vivid tale to inspire Hans

Sachs or impress itself for ever on the imagination of Heine. It is an account of a real episode in the struggle of Israel for a recognized place among the nations. It is a *Nahalat Abot*—an event whose meaning transcends the particular age and country in which it happened.

After discussing the book and the origin of the festival, we shall consider both the more interesting details of the ceremonial and the precise nature of the feast. The evolution of the medieval synagogue plays a part in our story. So, too, does the elaboration of a three day Purim in Jerusalem from the time when Nahmanides found its community to consist of two dark-skinned men; and no less the picturesque usage which today obtains in the land where first the festival took its name. Of great interest is the annual revival of the carnival which has come with the new life to Tel Aviv.

During the different periods of its growth the vast and still flourishing literature which the story of Esther inspired shows traces of the influence of prevailing fashions. First the Arab poetaster, then the *jongleur*, then parody itself dictate the form of expression. We shall deal separately with the Purim play, which appears to owe somewhat more to Gentile influences both in its origin and in its development than has popularly been supposed.

So rich a subject admits of no well-defined beginning or end. One can only select a few features for description, some verses for reproduction and some peculiarities for comment. So diverse are the Gentile opinions which have been expressed upon Purim, from the Emperor Honorius to Racine and to Professor Paton, and so free the hand with which a fond tradition has lavished customs on Purim, that it were idle for the historian to attempt to recapture the sentiment, the laughter and the glamor which the festival has gathered through the centuries. We shall be content if we have presented its endless diversity as elements of a developing whole, losing in the process a part of the charm which belongs to them as separate and individual events, but reflecting in its stead the central light which has endured.

CHAPTER I.

"I think for example of the extremely interesting question of the different elements of tradition, of the simple sagas and the associated sagas, which lie behind not only our existing books but behind the earliest written sources which it is reasonable to postulate. This is a fascinating if treacherous region; but it may yet be possible to discover with reasonable care paths to a better understanding of the Old Testament literature."

GEORGE BUCHANAN GRAY

PRESIDENTIAL ADDRESS TO THE
SOCIETY FOR OLD TESTAMENT
STUDY. JAN. 3, 1922.

CHAPTER I

THE BOOK AND THE ORIGIN OF THE FESTIVAL

Rabbi Judah bar Il'ai, a rabbi who flourished in the second century, was in many ways the model of the pious scholar. He relates how, while he was still a boy, he read the *megillah* to his teacher Rabbi Tarfon at Lud and that he was praised for his reading.[1] A small boy read the *megillah* before this same Rabbi Judah bar Il'ai at Usha some years later.[2] The boy was also named Judah but was later to be known as Judah ha-Nasi and to arrange a mishnaic collection which was to be authoritative. And Rabbi Meir, the great dialectician, tells how, when journeying in Asia Minor, Purim came upon him by surprise. He had with him no Hebrew copy of the book of Esther nor could one be obtained.[3] Meir had been a scribe and was fortunately able to write the book out by heart and

then to fulfill his religious obligations in
the prescribed manner.[4] A little later the
Palestinian amora, R. Joshua ben Levi,
maintained that the reading of the *megillah*
was one of the three things decreed by
the divine court.[5]

We cannot hope to emulate these rabbis,
whose deeds show so living an appreciation of the tale recounted in the *megillah*.[6]
In this book our appreciation is expressed
in a somewhat different manner which,
it is hoped, is none the less sincere if it be
more in keeping with the spirit of this age.
First the story is to be unfolded. Then
the book and the rabbinic evidence are
to be examined to establish as far as possible both its authorship and the date of
its composition. And lastly, whatever
relevant information can be gathered is
to be sifted in order to examine more
closely the nature and the origin of the
festival which Israel commemorates in
Purim.

The *megillah* (i. e. the scroll of Esther)
recounts[7] how Ahasuerus (old Persian

Khshayarshya; probably Xerxes, 485–464 B.C.E.) once gave a great banquet, first for his noblemen and then, democratically, for the people of Shushan (Susa), the capital city of his empire. On the last day of this feasting he ordered Vashti, his queen-elect, to come before his guests and to display her beauty before them. Vashti refused this indignity. In his great wrath Ahasuerus had her executed and justified his action by announcing in a royal edict to his whole empire that every man must be master in his own house. To fill Vashti's now vacant place all the most beautiful maidens in Persia were hastened to the king's palace in Shushan where, after twelve months of careful preparation, they were presented one by one to the gaze of the expectant king. The most comely of these maidens was Esther, the niece and adopted daughter of Mordecai, a Benjaminite living in Susa. Ahasuerus was overwhelmed by her beauty; and thus it came about that in the seventh year of his reign it was Esther

whom Ahasuerus chose to be his queen.
Shortly after her accession a conspiracy
was formed against the king's life by two
of the royal chamberlains.   Mordecai
discovered this plot and told it to Esther
who revealed it in Mordecai's name to
the king. The conspirators were straightway hanged and the story of Mordecai's
signal service to Ahasuerus was recorded
in the royal archives.

Some little time after, there rose to
power a certain Haman. The king raised
this noble's rank above that of his peers
and ordered all his meaner subjects to
abase themselves before the new vizier.
But Mordecai would not bow down except
before God, and publicly refused obeisance
to Haman.   Haman, smarting under
Mordecai's insult, conceived a great hatred
for the Jew and for his people. He sought
revenge, and succeeded in persuading the
king to publish throughout the Persian
Empire that on the thirteenth day of
Adar every Jew was to be slain and his
property confiscated. To choose the day

for the massacre of the Jews, Haman had cast lots—*purim*—from which the festival later took its name. The decree brought terror to the heart of every Jew in Persia. Mordecai, in duty to his race, acquainted Esther of it and induced her to intercede with the king on behalf of her people, the Children of Israel. In coming before the great king unsummoned, Esther risked the highest penalty of this wayward monarch's displeasure, but happily Ahasuerus forgave her presumption, and reaching out to her the golden scepter in token of his acquiescence, he promised to grant her whatever she might desire, even unto half of his kingdom. Esther asked only that he should come with Haman to her banquet. Ahasuerus accepted her invitation and at the feast asked her once more what might be her desire. Esther replied by craving the royal presence and that of his chief minister at yet another banquet. Haman departed from the palace rejoicing in his heart at this great honor done to him, but suddenly perceiving Mordecai

at the gate, his rejoicing turned forthwith
to wrath.   Mordecai in no way saluted
him.   When he reached home, Haman
revealed to his wife Zeresh both the tale
of honor and Mordecai's insult. She suggested to her husband that he should
erect gallows fifty cubits high on which
with the king's permission the hated
Mordecai might be strung up.   And
Haman did so.

That night the king could not sleep.
To pass the time more easily, he ordered
that the royal archives be brought and
read before him. Then, through the long
hours of the night, he heard how the
chamberlains had plotted against the
sacred life of the king and how Mordecai
in his wisdom and goodness had frustrated
their evil machinations. Ahasuerus, his
interest so vitally awakened, asked the
servants ministering to him the nature of
the reward which had been conferred upon
Mordecai for his loyal service. When he
learned that nothing had been done, he
turned to Haman who had just presented

himself at Court and asked him for his counsel. The king asked what should be done to the man whom the king delighted to honor. Haman, under the impression that these honors were intended for his own person, named only the very highest marks of royal approval, but to his intense chagrin he was commanded to bestow these dignities upon his enemy Mordecai. He did as the king bade him and hastened home with his head covered as in mourning to tell his wife and the company of his friends all that had befallen him. While Zeresh, after hearing her husband's woeful tale, was prophesying even worse things to come, the king's chamberlains arrived to escort Haman to Esther's second banquet.

When all these were assembled, Ahasuerus once more repeated his offer to Queen Esther, who on this occasion asked that her people might not be slain in cold blood. Now the king had forgotten the edict and asked her who had brought this danger upon the people of Israel.

When he learned that it was Haman who had been its author, he rose in anger and left the banqueting hall. Then, fearing for his life, Haman fell before the queen and prayed for mercy. The king returned suddenly, and seeing Haman bowed down on Esther's couch, his hands outstretched in pleading, thought that Haman was offering insult to her. One of the courtiers, Harbonah by name, gave the king a timely reminder that a gallows fifty cubits high was prepared in Haman's courtyard. On hearing this, Ahasuerus ordered Haman's immediate execution, and "then was the king's wrath pacified."

Mordecai was called before the king and installed in Haman's position, in token of which Ahasuerus gave him his signet ring. Esther continued her efforts to secure her people's safety. As the Persian laws did not allow a royal decree to be rescinded once it had been promulgated, Ahasuerus did all within his power by authorizing Mordecai to issue another edict. This proclamation, which was to

be made known throughout the whole
empire, announced that the Jews on the
day appointed for their destruction might
defend themselves from their assailants.

Thus it came to pass that when, on the
thirteenth of Adar, the Jews throughout
Persia were attacked by their neighbors,
they rose as one man and prevailed against
their enemies. In Susa alone they slew
five hundred on that day and hanged the
ten sons of Haman. Moreover Esther
gained the king's permission for her coun-
trymen in Susa to defend themselves on
the next day as well, when they slew some
three hundred Persians. In the provinces
of Persia seventy-five thousand Persians
were slain on the thirteenth of Adar, and
the fourteenth was celebrated as a day
of rejoicing, while in Susa it was the
fifteenth which was observed as a feast
day.

So mighty a salvation of the people of
Israel was naturally to be commemorated.
Esther and Mordecai sent out letters to
all the Jews in the hundred and twenty-

seven provinces of King Ahasuerus announcing that the fourteenth and fifteenth of Adar were to be held as "days of feasting and gladness, and of sending portions one to another, and gifts to the poor." The book closes with an account of the might and greatness of Mordecai, which was inscribed in the royal archives of the Medes and of the Persians.

Our narrative differs both in its simplicity and straightforwardness from the less lucid arguments not only of the higher critics but also of the Rabbis. The problems of date and authorship have proved fascinating to many generations of scholars, most especially to that generation which saw the deciphering of the cuneiform inscriptions and the consequent revealing not of one but of many Mesopotamian mythologies.

The doctors of the Talmud are chiefly interested in reconciling by subtle disputation the apparent inconsistencies in which, for the learned, both Bible and Mishna abound. As a general rule the form in

which the debate is couched is at once
simple and sprightly, the real difficulties
only being perceived when an attempt
is made to reconstruct a complete line
of argument.   There are never closely
defined agenda. Fortunately the evidence
which the Talmud adduces concerning
the book of Esther is more historical than
legal.

It was the unexpected mention of "a
second letter of Purim" (9.32) that so
vastly intrigued the Rabbis.[8]   "What
need could there have been for two letters?"
—they ask. Curiously enough three somewhat similar answers were propounded to
solve this enigma.   It was held by some
that when the first letter was received by
the Elders of the Great Synagogue, they
said heatedly: "Surely we have a sufficiency
of woes and of troubles, yet you would
add to them! Would you have us vaunt
ourselves in our victory over Haman?
Then surely the Gentiles will say that
none are more despicable than we are,
since we rejoice when they fall."   It was

in reply to this objection that a second letter was written pointing out that the first letter was already in the archives of the Medes and the Persians and that its publication in Israel could have no effect on relations with the Gentiles.

Other Rabbis held that the first letter was lost, in some unknown way. This is inferred from the fact that we find no *midrashim* (legends) based upon it! Esther therefore wrote "a second letter of Purim" which she sent to the Elders with the words: "Inscribe my story for all generations!" The Elders refused to accede to her request in a reply quoted by Resh Lakish: "Lo, I have written for the people of Israel the book divided into the Law, the Prophets and the Hagiographa, and not with four divisions, i. e. the Scrolls as well." (An interpretation of Prov. 22.20). This implies that the book of Esther, by virtue of its being a scroll, was not fit to be incorporated into the canon of the Old Testament. To this decision the Rabbis adhered until, reading on in the Bible, they came to the verse: "Inscribe this in a book for a memorial!" (Ex. 17.14). On this authority they accepted the scroll which Esther had written, rewrote it and included it in the canon.

This solution which the Rabbis wove on a woof of biblical verses is rewoven in the Palestinian Talmud into a somewhat more ornate fabric. We learn there that Rabbi Samuel bar Nahman in the name of Rabbi Jonathan said that Esther's message came before a council of eighty-five Elders of whom thirty were prophets. All were deeply grieved, and raising their voice in lamentation said: "Moses spake unto us saying, 'From now on no prophet has authority to introduce any new thing to you'." But God gave light to their eyes and reading on in the Bible they came to the passage: "Inscribe this in a book for a memorial" (Ex. 17.14), and were able to accept the history of Esther as holy.

All three solutions have one feature in common; they reveal a real doubt whether

the book was to be accepted into the canon
of the Old Testament or not. Elsewhere
the Rabbis continue to record their con-
troversies in less imaginative but more
vital discussion.[9] Was the book of Esther
so holy that it might be said *Metamme
et ha-yadayim* (it requires ritual cleanliness
of the reader)? Those who reject it say
that it was not inspired by the Holy One
blessed be He, if only for the reason that
the name of God does not occur even once
in the book. For this fact two explanations
are offered. One is that Mordecai, know-
ing that his account would be translated
into Persian for the king's records, took
care not to introduce the name of God
lest it be rendered by some abomination;
and the other, that the book of Esther
was translated by the men of the Great
Synagogue from the Persian into the
Hebrew, and it was impossible that the
name of God should occur in the Persian.
Our Cabalists are faced with no such
difficulty. They see the name of God in
the title *melek* (king) which occurs one

hundred and eighty-four times in the *megillah*, wherein they follow the lead of the writers of the *midrashim*, who interpreted this word, when unqualified by a following "Ahasuerus," as referring to God.

Krochmal,[10] a great Jewish scholar of the nineteenth century who draws his inspiration exclusively from Jewish sources, concludes that our book of Esther is the second letter, not only written in Hebrew but also inspired by God. In his view it was the first letter written in Aramaic which was lost.

That the sanctity of the book of Esther should have been a cause of contention is hardly surprising, for the book is scarcely an account of God's dealings with man but only an explanation of a festival of the Persian Jews. One is safe, however, in concluding from these arguments that down to a comparatively late period there was no unanimity of rabbinic opinion as to whether Esther was a fit book to be incorporated into the canon of the Old

Testament. Moreover the fact that the tractate Megillah in the Talmud, after discussing the sanctity of the book continues with a fanciful commentary upon it, establishes a precedent for the elaboration of the scroll of Esther in later times.

In his article entitled *Purim und Parodie*,[11] which the learned Moritz Steinschneider published in 1902, he gave his opinion of the then recent advances in the "higher criticism" of the book of Esther. He says: ". . . worüber erst eine Studie über die Geschichte dieses Festes Aufschluss geben kann, während in neuerer Zeit nur christliche Gelehrte über Ursprung und Namen von Purim in Verbindung mit der höheren kritik über das Buch Esther Forschungen angestellt, auch seltsame Hypothesen aufgestellt haben, die ich—dahingestellt sein lasse . . ."

Today there is an even vaster array of hypotheses perhaps to be left unconsidered. They come from the pens of those higher critics who find in Esther an everflowing source of discussion. Many are

the scholars who have valiantly attempted
to explain the difficulties which the narrative involves. From their theses it
becomes increasingly clear that the prob
lems of date and authorship of the book
of Esther can scarcely be adequately considered unless some solution is arrived at
to the problem of the origin of the festival.
The purpose of the book is patent to the
most casual reader—it is to account for
the institution and to promote the celebration of the Purim festival. But before we
can permit ourselves to enter into the
maze of higher critical sources and origins
it would be well to point out a few of the
inconsistencies in the book itself which
make it difficult, not to say impossible,
to accept Esther at its face value.

We are told by Herodotus[12] that a certain Xerxes, who reigned from 485 to 464
in Persia, was the tallest and most hand-
some man in the Persian host, but that
in character he was a cowardly and cruel
tyrant. If this is the impulsive despot who
is to be identified with the Ahasuerus of

the book of Esther, it seems a little unlikely that so proud a monarch should accept a captive as his queen and a Jew as his prime minister. Moreover the edict of Haman commanding the massacre of all the Jews would surely have met with opposition from the other Persian satraps. To accept as an historical event the second edict of Mordecai, which plunged the empire into civil strife, is so strange that one is surprised that Ahasuerus should ratify it; and if it did gain royal approval, one is still surprised that no other historical records corroborate our story. When Esther was chosen to be queen it is said that she did not reveal her Jewish origin though she was apparently known to be the niece of Mordecai the Jew. Stranger still is the assumption that Mordecai and Esther could continue in close communication with one another when Esther was already in the harem of Ahasuerus. Haman describes the Jews as being dispersed throughout all the provinces of the kingdom of Persia and as being disobedient to the king's laws. But in the Persian period the Jews, so far as can be inferred from other sources, were not scattered throughout the provinces, nor is there any record to show that they were rebellious, though this latter may well have been a lie fabricated by Haman to strengthen his own position and to secure the destruction of his hated enemies. The picture of Persian manners and customs presents inconsistencies with such facts as are known. Generally speaking they convey the atmosphere of a fairy tale rather than that of sober reality, even the fantastic reality of the Persian Court.

Such are the improbabilities and inconsistencies which lay the historical character of the book open to grave doubts. Of the critics, Josephus[13] assigned the book to the reign of Artaxerxes the first, with whom he identifies Ahasuerus; Philo ascribes the book to the High Priest Joachim; Augustine held that Ezra was its author; while the Talmud, in a passage already referred to,[14] says that the Men of the Great Synagogue wrote the book. And many of the critics who have doubted the historical character of Esther have nevertheless held that the festival took its origin in some Jewish victory, for otherwise there is no sufficient reason why the festival should have been included in the sacred calendar. Thus Bleek[15] suggested that it marks the end of the Babylonian exile, while Willrich,[16] wandering still deeper in the labyrinth of Jewish history in the Greek period, sees in the book an allegorical interpretation of the fate of Israel in 48 B.C.E. in Egypt under the Ptolemies. In 1772 Michaelis[17] put forward the view that Purim was founded to commemorate the victory of Judas Maccabaeus over Nicanor on the thirteenth day of Adar 161 B.C.E. He holds that the name of the festival is to be derived from the Hebrew *purah* (wine press) in some such phrase as that in Isaiah, chapter 63, where the word is used in a description of God vanquishing his enemies: "I trod down the wine press (*purah*) alone . . .

and their (i. e. my enemies') life-juice
splashed forth."

Nor was Michaelis the last to see in
Esther a product of Greek Coele-Syria.
The profound historian Graetz[18] allows
his fancy to roam perhaps a little too freely
over the later Greek period in seeking out
a time which should mirror in its feeling
that outlook which is reflected in the book
of Esther.   He came to the conclusion
that the most likely epoch for the composition of the book was that of the per-
secutions of Antiochus Epiphanes, and
that the festival was a Jewish version
of the Greek feast of *Pithoigia* or cask-
opening, a season of wine drinking and
sending of presents like the *Vinalia* of
the Romans.   He thinks that in all probability the custom was introduced by a
tax gatherer in the reign of Ptolemy
Philopator (225–205 B.C.E.).

The evidence which has led so many
critics on the path of error may be grouped
as follows.   The verse: "and Mordecai
wrote these things" (9.20), does not refer,

as Clement of Alexandria maintained, to the whole book but only to the letter which follows. Otherwise no reference is made in Esther either to the book itself or to its author. No writer before the beginning of the Christian era mentions the book, not even Ben Sira (c. 170 B.C.E.) who gives a list of the great Jews of the past. Purim is mentioned first in the second book of Maccabees under the name of "Mordecai Day," and next in Josephus, which seems to indicate that Purim was not kept by the Palestinian Jews before the first century B.C.E. The halo of romance cast upon the Persian empire, the scattered Jews and the conversion of multitudes to Judaism (8.17, 9.27) is typical rather of the background of the Greek period. The absence of any theological trend in the book, the lack of any Messianic hope, the strong hatred of the enemies of Israel, the spirit of independence, all seem to be in keeping rather with the spirit of the Jews in the Greek period. And lastly the language of the

book and the style in which it is written
point to a late date. In the view of certain
critics, the author is so strongly influenced
by Aramaic that his Hebrew is both
awkward and labored. He seems to have
written his work at a period when Hebrew
was no longer the vernacular of the Jews,
but only the language of the sacred books.

But even if one allows that Esther
belongs in its present form to the third
or even to the second century B. C. E.,
this does not exclude the possibility that
the story originated in Persia and was
handed down by oral tradition till it was
written for all time to explain the feast
of Purim. Graetz has inspired many
scholars to search through the Greek
period for an event which might serve as
a peg on which to hang the book of Esther.
Kuenen's precise 130 B.C.E. can hardly
inspire credence, more especially as a
further study of the festival in the light
of new knowledge leads us to take its
origin back to a more remote date.

All the more recent solutions of the

problem of the date of the composition of the book of Esther are inextricably bound up with the solution of the problem of the origin of the festival which it was written to institute.

The rivers of scholarship, like the ancient rivers of Eden, flow for Purim through four lands: Greece, Palestine under Hellas, Persia and Babylon. The Grecian *wady* of the *Pithoigia* is lost in the sands of the desert of improbability quite near its source, for though it is conceivable that certain Grecian customs may have influenced the mode of Purim observance, yet the evidence that Purim takes its origin in the *Pithoigia* is too scanty to convince. Hatred for Greece and incompatibility of religious conceptions were far too prevalent in ancient Israel to permit of conscious syncretism.

It was Paul Haupt[19] in his lecture on Purim who showed most convincingly how the river flows through Israel under Hellas. In his peroration he says: "I believe therefore that Purim is derived from the old Persian equivalent of Vedic '*purti*' (portion). Purim, 'portions, gifts' (Hebrew *manoth* Esther 9. 19, 22) corresponds to the Latin '*strenae*,' French '*etrennes*!' The explanation of *Yeme |Purim* as 'Days of the Lots' is a subsequent popular etymology suggested by the Hebrew word for 'portion' in the sense of 'lot, destiny' as well as by oracular practices observed on New Year's Eve. The book of Esther, just as the book of Judith, is a festal legend for the feast of Purim; it is not a historical book, or a historical novel, but entirely fictitious. The incidents related were suggested by the sufferings of the Jews during the Syrian persecutions and their glorious victory over Nicanor on the thirteenth of Adar 161 B.C.E. Nicanor is the prototype of Haman and the honors bestowed on Mordecai correspond to the distinctions conferred on the Maccabee high-priest Jonathan, the younger brother and successor of Judas Maccabeus. The names of Haman and Vashti are Susian or Elamite, while Mordecai and Esther correspond to the Babylonian Marduk and Ishtar. The antagonism between Haman and Vashti (sic) on the one hand, and Mordecai and Esther on the other, may have been suggested by an ancient Babylonian festal legend celebrating a victory gained by the chief god of Babylon over the principal deity of the Elamites; and this may ultimately be a nature-myth symbolizing the victory of the deities of Spring over the frost giants of Winter who hate the sunshine and always plot to bring back Winter to the earth, just as the frost-giants of Jötunheim in old Norse mythology hated the beautiful god Balder, with whose presence Summer came back to the ice-bound earth. Mordecai, the god of the vernal sun, triumphed over the frost-giant Haman, who was a braggart like Hrungner, the strongest of the giants in Jötunheim, and the winter of Judah's discontent and oppression was made glorious summer by the sun of Judas Maccabeus."

To find in a secular festival some hidden

harmony with the cycle of nature must attract even the least imaginative of students. But Paul Haupt seems to have allowed his vast learning to lead him astray. He has overlooked certain issues which though superficially unimportant are none the less vital. Nicanor's day is the 13th of Adar, not the 14th, which is distinct from it and known as Mordecai Day. There is no counterpart to Esther in the events of the Maccabean period. If the feast owes its inception to a Jewish victory, the corresponding myth would hardly be based on a Babylonian festal legend. Paul Haupt's derivation of the name "Purim" would indicate an old Persian origin, while the Elamitish discord of Haman and Vashti and the Babylonian symphony of Marduk and Ishtar are, to say the least, difficult. His position, in short, is not tenable.

It will be remembered that one of the rivers flowed through Persia. Since the scene of the book of Esther is laid in that country and since the book contains a number of Persian words and allusions to Persian customs, it seems natural to examine Persian evidence. Meier, Hitzig, Fürst and Meijboom[20] all identify Purim with the Persian New Year festival. The names in the book of Esther are mythological; Haman is the same as the Sanskrit "heman," winter; Esther is "sthara," the star par excellence, the sun; and Mordecai "mard chaya," melter of shadow. And thus the story of Esther depicts the victory of the gods of summer over the gods of winter. Quite apart from the philological objections, this theory is hardly attractive. A more developed identification which gained wider acceptance was with the Persian festival in memory of the dead, called *Farvardigan* and referred to in the sixth century by Menander as *Furdigan*. Both Lagarde and Renan identified an inferred late Persian *Fourdi* =Aramaic *Purday* =earlier Hebrew *Purdim* =later Hebrew *Purim*. The derivation from *Pur* =*lot*, was dismissed as a textual corruption.

It was left to Schwally[21] to throw over this rather impossible etymology and to adopt only the parallel of the *Farvardigan* or cult of the dead, a cult which, he says, stood midway between Yahwism and heathenism and which was practiced in Israel from the earliest times. The Purim banquets are funeral feasts and the presents are offerings to the dead. He quotes the legend which was current in early medieval Jewry in Persia which al-Beruni, the Arab geographer, recorded and which Sachau has translated. It tells how at one period Haman sat by the entrance to the graveyard and exacted three and a half *dirhems* for every corpse. But Schwally, one fears, is yet another scholar who, impelled by the eerie elusiveness of the Purim festival, has left behind him cold reasoned argument and embarked for the realms of fantasy. It is not likely that a vague cult of the dead which may have prevailed in ancient Israel should persist in the later Purim. His evidence is too insubstantial and his Plutonian pageant too faded to build thereon Purim's cloud-capp'd towers.

We must follow the course of the fourth river.

Fritz Hommel, Zimmern, Jensen, Nowack, Meissner, Winckler and Toy[22] agree in tracing Purim and the Esther legend to a Babylonian source. Mordecai is Marduk, the chief god of the Babylonian pantheon. Esther is Ishtar, the chief goddess, and her other name Hadassah is the Assyrian *Hadashshatu* which means "myrtle," then "bride," and is often used as the title of a goddess. Both in the Talmud and in the *Targum Sheni* the Rabbis refer to Esther as the star Ishtar or Venus whose beauty is beyond compare. Haman is Humman or Humban, the chief god of the Elamites and a solar deity, and this identification is perhaps confirmed by the Jewish legend that he had three hundred and sixty-five counselors, as many as the days of the solar year. Vashti is held to be Mashti, an Elamite goddess, and Zeresh either Girisha or Siris. This would base the story on a recorded conflict of Marduk and Ishtar with the Elamite deities Humman, Vashti and Girisha or Siris. It was this general theory which so attracted Paul Haupt. The exact festival on which Purim is based is not, however, stated.

Jensen found the prototype of the Esther legend in the Assyrian Gilgamesh epic, where Gilgamesh, the sun-god and counterpart of Marduk, conquers Humbaba (i. e. Humman or Humban) the king of Elam with the aid of *Kallatu* (the bride) or Hadassah. Humbaba is the guardian of a lofty cedar, Haman's gallows, which belongs to the goddess Irwina (= Ishtar). In the book of Esther, however, it is Esther who is the heroine and overthrower of Haman whereas here it is Ishtar who is the enemy of Gilgamesh—the counterpart of Mordecai. To overcome these inconsistencies Gunkel explained Esther as an allegory of the struggle between the gods of Babylonia and those of Elam and not directly to be connected with the

Gilgamesh epic. The prominence given to Esther in our story is due, he says, to the fact that the city of Ishtar and not the city of Marduk was the leader in the struggle. This is based on insufficient evidence.

The assyriologist Zimmern turned to the creation myth to solve our problem. Humman and Vashti, the gods of the Elamites, represent the gods of chaos, while Marduk and Ishtar are order and light, who by their victory bring peace and prosperity to the world. Here, once more, it is another scholar who comes forward with a solution of the prominence of Esther. Bruno Meissner conjectures that in later times Ishtar may have risen higher in the popular esteem and ousted Marduk from his throne. There is, however, no definite evidence that this took place.

It was left for Winckler to seek an origin for Purim in the third great Assyrian epic, the Tammuz-Ishtar legend, a poem which tells how spring brings new life to

dead nature. Haman the Agagite (=
"wrathful" from the Assyrian root *agagu*)
is the deposed sun-god who dies annually
in the accepted manner of solar heroes.
Vashti, who is none other than the virgin
Ishtar, disobeys the king's command
because his reign on earth is over, and
while she and Haman are in the under-
world, their terrestrial counterparts Esther
and Mordecai rule in their place. Ahasuerus
is the abiding element before whom con-
tradictory nature is reconciled.

All these myths have in common one
feature. Though superficially they are
attractive as parallels to the Esther legend,
none but the biassed can see in them an
origin for Purim. It is left for us to cruise
about the sea of the festal calendars of
Mesopotamia.

Lagarde abandoned his *Farvardigan*
theory[23] and turned for a derivation of the
name Purim to the Mandean *puhra*, a
meal. In the same year Fritz Hommel
sought in the Assyrian *puhru*, assembly,
an origin for Purim. It was Zimmern

who pointed out that *puhru* was only one
name of the Babylonian New Year feast
which is also called by the Sumerian name
Zagmuk (beginning of the year), when the
gods assembled together and determined
the fates of men for the ensuing year by
means of tablets of fate or lots. The same
is recorded of the Jewish New Year.
Thus the lots of Haman are traced to their
ultimate source and the banqueting is a
record of the fact that the gods became
drunk at the feast of creation.

But *puhru* cannot by normal philology
become Purim, nor is it likely that the
Zagmuk festival celebrated in the first
two weeks of Nisan, already parallel with
the Jewish New Year, should become
Purim of the fourteenth and fifteenth of
Adar. Once more Bruno Meissner modifies
the view put forward by Zimmern and
holds that Purim reaches Israel through
the Persian offspring of the Babylonian
Zagmuk. This child is known to Strabo
and Berossus as *Sakaia*. This is the Bacchanalian festival when Ishtar, goddess

of love, was omnipotent, when a mock king was enthroned over the populace, and when all the social relations were reversed. It is thought, therefore, that Purim records the annual freedom of the Jews of Susa while Ishtar reigned. In *The Golden Bough*, Frazer develops this interpretation and is of the opinion that during the *Sakaia* the mock king and queen impersonated the god and goddess of winter, whose death, at the end of the feast, marked the coming of spring. Mordecai and Esther are the god and the goddess of fertility, who come to life again at the beginning of the New Year. This view postulates a more intimate connection between Purim and the spring festival than the biblical story allows. None the less, it is possible the *Sakaia* may have partly inspired the Purim festival.

Strabo (born 63 B.C.E.) says in his *Geography* (ch. 512): "There were found sanctuaries both of Anaitis and of the associated gods Oman and Anadatos,

Persian divinities (δαιμόνων); and they
celebrated a festival and yearly rites,
namely the *Sakaia*." Anaitas has been
identified with the old Iranian deity
Anahita (the undefiled), the goddess of
love and beauty. When in the sixth century B.C.E. or possibly earlier, the cults
of Babylon became known to the Persians,
she was immediately identified with Ishtar.
Strabo is wrong in ascribing to Cyrus
the institution of the festival in honor of
Anaitis. He affirms that it was, however,
a carnival. Athenaeus, quoting Berossus
(circa 250 B.C.E. in the *Dipnosophistiae*,
ch. 639) says that the *Sakaia* was celebrated at Babylon on the sixteenth of
Loos (=Ab) when a king of misrule,
Zogane (Mishnaic Hebrew *Segan* =repre-
sentative), was appointed and the social
order reversed. Dion Chrysostom (345–
407 C.E.) records that the festival was
Persian in origin and that a malefactor
was put on the king's throne to rule during
the festival and to be scourged and hanged
afterwards.

Langdon suggests[24] that the "carnival of the Lord of Misrule was most probably held at the autumnal New Year festival from most remote antiquity in honor of the marriage of the god Ningirsu and the goddess Bau at Lagash, and in honor of the queen of love, Ishtar, at Erech. At the latter seat of one of Sumer's most ancient cults the festival survived until the last century before our era, and it was from there that the carnival passed into Persia under the patronage of Anaitis." He derives the name *Sakaia* from *Um Sakkuti*, "the day of fools" or the like, and maintains that the festival is composite, being in part derived from the yearly adbication of the king for a short period and in part from the conquest of the spring sun over the winter season. Here, in his view, is the source of the Purim festivities. He establishes the derivation of the name Purim from the use of the word *Puru* in the sense of "lot," a loan-word from Sumerian, where it means "a stone bowl."

Yet conscious borrowing of heathen rites must have been repugnant to Jews of any age. It is true that Jewish custom has been shown to be largely syncretistic,[25] and that normal analogy illustrates a regular folk motif parading in the guise of a Jewish miracle. Nevertheless the tradition which takes the festival back to Persia seems to be a true one. It remains more than likely that the spirit of carnival reached Israel from Iran long before the Greek period; as we have seen, the Jews of Persia had full opportunity to join in the annual revelry of their neighbors. Later they may have selected for their reviling the god Omanos in Haman and just conceivably Anadatos in Hammedatha. Moreover the other names in Esther are best explained by Scheftelowitz as Aryan in derivation.

Tradition, though founded on facts, tends to distort them for its own ends. It is the task of the student to distinguish between distortion and original fact. The explanations of the origin of Purim from

Assyrian sources have accounted neither for all the important events nor for all the important characters in our story. That a satisfying and direct Assyrian explanation would not be forthcoming might well have been foreseen. One has but to compare the creation legends of Israel and Assyria to see a clear disparity. Much is similar, but a complete identification is impossible.

It is hardly possible that a festival sacrifice should be instituted in Persia and not in the Holy Land. In accordance with the secular character of the book of Esther, there is mention neither of any religious observance nor of gratitude to God for the deliverance of Israel. Thus, in spite of the adoption of Purim into the religious calendar, the secular nature of the festival has remained the distinctive feature of its celebration throughout its history.

The Talmud does however hint at the nature of its origin. Rabbi Samuel bar Judah seems to have had an inkling of the early history of the festival. He says that Purim was first instituted in Susa but spread later to the diaspora. The date of its introduction to Palestine cannot be determined with any exactitude. There is a note at the end of a Greek manuscript of Esther[26] which states that the translation of the "Purim Epistle," the work of Lysimachus son of Ptolemaeus of Jerusalem, was introduced into Egypt in the fourth year of Ptolemy and Cleopatra. It is possible only to guess which Ptolemy and Cleopatra the author had in mind. Some scholars favor Philometor (181–145 B.C.E.), others Soter (Lathyrus, 114 B.C.E.), and so the historical value of the note remains dubious, but in view of the reference to Purim in the Mishna (see infra) the former seems the more likely.

All the various higher critical accounts of the origin of the Purim festival are so conflicting and confused that it is difficult to accept any one of them as authoritative. Above all they seem to evade the difficulty of explaining the lapse of time between the adoption by the Jews of the festival and the date by which the Jews had compiled their own legends and sincerely believed that Esther and Mordecai were historical personages. That Jews living in Persia should have Persian or Assyrian names, and even names which resemble those of local deities, is hardly surprising. It is as though a higher critic of some future millenium who found a Jew named Siegfried in some Judeo-German novel should identify him with the hero of early Teutonic mythology. Though the Rabbis tell us that the Jews of Egypt owed their deliverance to the fact that they changed neither their Hebrew language nor their Jewish names, we are not bound to assume the same constancy in the Jewish captives within the Persian Empire. It is not unfair, in view of the inconclusive nature of the critical arguments, to re-assess such material as is to be found in rabbinic literature. That all the rabbinic references and discussions of Purim are based on a quibble with regard to the second letter of Esther seems an

overstatement; and we may justifiably
assume that the Rabbis were preserving
and echoing genuine Jewish tradition when
they re-argued the problem of the can-
onicity of Esther, and that on one occasion
the Persian Jews were saved from disaster
in a way which a people who believed in
an omnipotent Deity who had chosen
them for His peculiar people, could think
of only as miraculous. They celebrated
this salvation in Persian fashion. The
deliverance occurred on the fourteenth of
Adar and was either made known on or
extended to the fifteenth of that month
in Susa. So signal an event could not be
allowed to sink into oblivion. In all likeli-
hood a letter was written to the Jewish
authorities in Jerusalem to tell them what
had taken place in Persia. The papyri
found at Elephantine in Upper Egypt
afford a precedent and a parallel.[27] The
chief of this community of Jews in Yeb
writes to the high-priest in Jerusalem.
He tells how the Egyptians had risen up
against them and destroyed their temple.

He appeals for funds to rebuild their house of worship that they may continue to serve the Lord.

We know from the talmudic sources that the more conservative Elders of Jerusalem were taken aback when they received the letter from Esther and Mordecai. The institution of Purim would conflict with the fundamental principle that the Law of Moses was complete, that no prophet should introduce any innovation; yet here were Esther and Mordecai trying to do that very thing. The progress of the discussion which ensued has already been narrated. It is sufficient to recall that by the time when Second Maccabees was written Adar 14th had become a festival day. By mishnaic times the festival was generally observed—The Mishna Rosh Hashanah speaks of sending out messengers to see the new moon for Adar in order to fix the day of Purim while Megillah is devoted exclusively to the festival. By talmudic times Purim was established—*misheniknas adar marbim besimhah.*

In the light of what has gone before it can hardly be too rash to assume that our festival saw its birth in Persia. Eagerly assimilating pagan modes, it passed its childhood in Persia from the end of the fourth to the beginning of the third century, and was adopted in Palestine during that century. Here its fosterparents took so kindly to it that their enthusiasm spread to the Jews of the most distant parts of the diaspora until they too began to join in happy celebration. At the latest the book as we know it was written at the beginning of the third century. Its author was no mean artist. Not only did he tell his tale well, but he improved it in the telling. He did not hesitate to paint his narrative with the bright colors of Assyrian legend, nor did he refrain from advising Israel to imitate their neighbors and send gifts to one another. The Persian New Year festival was refreshing and pleasant. He hoped that Purim would be still happier and more characteristically Jewish. The gifts may be imitations of New Year gifts, *étrennes*, and the names may be echoes of nature myths, but the story is a Jewish one.

It may have been somewhat in this wise that a pagan spring carnival, marked in its remoter parentage by the ironical crowning of a buffoon king, followed by his scourging and death, traveled from Erech, the old Babylonian center, to Persia and from Persia back to Babylon, subtly to be woven into the fabric of our story.

Henceforth in Israel the Purim festival is a season of joy and of merry-making; some of its legends seem to recall Mesopotamian myths, and wherever it goes it tends always to adopt the trappings of similar pagan jestings; otherwise its origin has long lost itself in the harmonious story of the beautiful Jewish queen who saved her people from destruction.

CHAPTER II.

"The local community is the real unit of Jewish life, the group of persons living in close proximity to each other having its centre and focus in the synagogue . . . So long as the community could hold together there was a haven of refuge for its harassed members, there they could find the solace and strength of their religion and live their own life unmocked by the hard and cruel world. The Jew found the only freedom for the higher life of the spirit in the synagogue . . ."

R. TRAVERS HERFORD.

CHAPTER II

THE SYNAGOGUE SERVICE
AND THE MEGILLAH

The distinction between religion and ritual is not a fundamental one. In spite of the fervid denunciations of Amos and Hosea, Zechariah's proclamations of God's love for His creatures, and Isaiah's optimistic teachings, Israel has for the most part retained the shadow and not the substance of their religion. And this shadow, this ritual of the synagogue, has a beauty of its own, a concreteness and a suggestiveness which can captivate the simple mind more easily than the abstract ideality of a system of pure ethics.

Though the more salient features of the service of the synagogue go back to talmudic times, the synagogues of today are not direct descendants of those which Dr. Sukenik has recently excavated in Palestine;[28] the permutation through which they went during the Middle Ages is such that the original elements are not easily discerned in the developed whole. At a time when the Jews had no leisure for calculated agnosticism, when they were compelled for their own safety to live penned together within the walls of a ghetto, mostly in poverty, and constantly in danger of losing not only their property but also their lives, they made the synagogue ritual an end in itself, and elaborated it until it finally took on those forms which are now current. For these Jews, who wrote many of our prayers, the study of Judaism was the only means of escape from the surrounding darkness, and every rabbinic argument was considered fascinating and profound in direct proportion to the complexity, compression and subtlety of its expression.

The synagogue became a house of meeting and study as much as of worship. The children were brought to it as to a second home in order to join in the ritual dear to their parents so that they, by learning to love the synagogue in their youth, should in maturer years come to hold the *vita Judaica*[29] as the sole end of life.

These were the men who fostered the ancient spirit of revelry in Purim by giving new life to jejune talmudic aphorisms. They were the first to sing in chorus certain verses of the book of Esther for the special delight of the children;[30] a custom which now has the validity of law. For them Purim was a brief season of joy and exultation, a rare occasion for the display of humor in a life, which to judge from the *'Emek ha-Baka*, was singularly free from light-hearted moments.

It is true that Purim has in England lost that abandon which used to be, and in some countries still is, a signal feature of this festival. Yet though the hasidic brandy and salt herring are not looked on with favor in all synagogues today, it is worth recording that an eighteenth century congregation in London had to call in the watch to prevent itself from making too much noise during the reading

of the *megillah*.[31] The present formality
of the service is best explained by the
saying: *Wie die Christen so die Juden*.[32]
Moreover, as we shall see, there are still
congregations where Purim brings freedom
and humor, and this particular heritage
from the Middle Ages is not forgotten.

The first duty of Purim is prescribed
in a tractate of the Talmud called Megillah.[33] On the fourteenth of Adar the book
of Esther must be publicly read. Rabbi
Joshua ben Levi of the third century C.E.
maintains that a further reading is to take
place on the eve of Purim. The women
are to be present since the feast celebrates
deliverance wrought by a woman. A conflict of opinion is recorded in the Mishna:
Whereas Rabbi Judah holds that the reading of chapter 2 verse 5 to the end is all
that is necessary, there are others who
hold that the reading of chapter 3 verse 7
or even chapter 6 verse 7 to the end is
sufficient. Against all these Rabbi Meir
contends that the whole of the book is to
be read, a view which is confirmed on page

19b of the tractate, and later by general practice. There are certain congregations, however, where it is customary to read the first six chapters on the first Sabbath evening in Adar and the rest on the following Sabbath evening, while elsewhere the book is read entirely on the second Sabbath.

It is interesting to note that according to the Mishna Megillah (30a), talking during the recitation of the book of Esther was strictly forbidden. One infers that even in mishnaic times discipline on the day of Purim was lax. The Mishna is careful to recall that on *Shabbat Zakor* (i. e. the Sabbath before Purim) the lesson from Torah is Exodus chapter 17 verses 8 to 16, which describes an attack of the Amalekites upon the Jews. In Esther Haman is called the Agagite and Agag is referred to elsewhere as the king of the Amalekites, the eternal enemies of the Jewish people; hence it came about that, in the eyes of the Rabbis, Haman and Amalek are identified. Nor does the Mishna

make mention of the blessings now intoned
before and after the public recitation of
the book. The custom takes its origin in
a talmudic prescription. Furthermore, the
Talmud in Megillah 16b states that the
names of the ten sons of Haman (9.7–10)
are to be read in one breath as a record
of their simultaneous execution.

Benjamin, a scribe of 13th century
France, enumerates the duties of Purim
as they were observed in his days. In
a Jewish vade-mecum (British Museum
Add. 11639) he gives a selection from
Rabbi Yehudai's (Gaon of Sura 760)
Halakot le-Purim or "Laws for the Observance of Purim," from which one gathers
that the ritual which obtains to-day was
already practiced in his time. Yehudai
Gaon institutes a comparison between
Hanukkah and Purim and proceeds to
enumerate the blessings which are intoned
before and after the reading of the *Megillah*.
William Schickart in his speech before the
Doctors of Tübingen on February 14, 1634,
describes these blessings impressively:

"Tres preculas demurmurat praecentor; unam, quia digni sint habiti haec sacra tractare; alteram, quod miraculose majores olim Deus conservavit; tertiam, quod huc usque vixerunt ad eam festivitatem." (The reader chants three short prayers: one that they are held worthy to read the sacred book; second, that God miraculously delivered their ancestors in those days; third, that they are in life to celebrate this festival.)

There was apparently still divided opinion in medieval France concerning the recitation of the blessing after the *Megillah*. Some stopped at the phrase: "Blessed art thou, O Lord, who on behalf of Thy people Israel, metest out punishment to all their adversaries, O God our Savior," while others went on with a *piyyut* attributed in the *Mahzor Vitry* to the Men of the Great Synagogue. Today, the continuation, which is to be found in the standard prayer book, is read only at the evening service. For the rest Yehudai Gaon emphasizes the importance of the evening meal or *se'udah*, which must commence while there is yet daylight; next he expounds the law concerning the duties of one traveling before Purim, and finally describes the scroll of Esther ritually suitable for synagogue reading. It would appear from his selected *Duties of Purim* that the medieval French synagogue was either badly ventilated or too well heated. "If in the course of his reading the *Megillah*," quotes Benjamin, "a man should become drowsy, and the congregation call his attention to this and the reader himself remember where he left off, this does not constitute an offence; on the other hand if he should fall asleep and has to be reminded where he was, this does constitute an offence."

Benjamin has shrewdly avoided doubtful issues by confining his attention to accepted decisions; the fuller text of Yehudai's laws is to be found in the *Mahzor Vitry*. But the fertile seed of talmudic injunction was to grow into the flourishing tree of later observance. It was during

the gaonic period,[34] just after the close of
the canon of the Talmud, that the custom
arose for the whole congregation to join
in reciting those verses which tell of
Mordecai's origin (2.5) and of his triumph
(8.15, 16; 10.3). Saadia Gaon, who is
remembered apart from his polemical
writings for his translation of the Bible
into Arabic, held that only chapter 2
verse 5 and chapter 8 verse 15 were to
be read by the whole congregation.

There is good reason to believe that the
fast—*Ta'anit Ester*[35]—was also instituted
about this time. This typically Jewish
institution is explained by the Rabbis as
a commemoration of the fast of Esther,
Mordecai and the people of Israel, recorded
in chapter 4 verse 16. But Rabbi Aha of
Shabha who flourished in the eighth century is the first to mention it. In explaining
Esther chapter 9 verse 8: "The thirteenth
was the time of gathering," he says that
"gathering" can only connote prayer and
fasting. Moreover whereas some, especially those Jews who live east of Suez,

are wont to fast rigorously on the thirteenth, others in Eastern Europe fast on the first and second Monday and Thursday following Purim and follow the law which the Rabbis of Palestine in the eighteenth century laid down in the *Masseket Soferim.*

Qui s'excuse s'accuse. Rabbi Aha's defence is too far-fetched. The variety of modes in which the fast is observed of itself suggests that it may have for its origin nothing more than a specialization of the periodic Monday and Thursday fasts. Furthermore Esther did not fast in Adar but in Nisan. There is, it is true, a general law which forbids fasting in Nisan, but if it was this law which was the cause of the change in date the Talmud would surely have given warning.

It is best to class this fast as a *Minhag be'alma*—a universal custom. For the Jew of Aden and the Jew of Teheran it is as serious as that on the Day of Atonement. The fast is naturally wearying and if the thirteenth should happen to fall on a Sabbath it is put back to the previous

Thursday in order that time be allowed for ample preparations for Purim.

It would be illogical to describe further the modes of Purim observance before the date of Purim is adequately discussed. According to the Bible story the slaughter of the Persians which came to an end in the provinces on the fourteenth of Adar did not cease in Shushan till the fifteenth. In order to give the towns of Palestine the same rank as that of Shushan the Talmud states that in those towns which are known to have been walled from the days of Joshua the son of Nun, the fifteenth— *Shushan Purim*—is to be the feast day. A little known variation based on this ruling is the *Purim ha-Meshullash* or "the three day Purim."[36] This long festival is peculiar to Jerusalem, where it is celebrated at distant intervals. This took place in 1930, which saw Purim in Jerusalem on the fourteenth, fifteenth and sixteenth of Adar, viz., Friday, Saturday and Sunday; the next occasion on which this will occur is 1950. For the rest, in different periods the interval varies from three to four, to seven and even to twenty years. The elaboration follows naturally on the fact that at these intervals the fifteenth of Adar falls on a Saturday; the fourteenth can never fall on this day.

When the fifteenth of Adar falls on a Saturday, Friday's duties are the reading of the *Megillah*, the sending of gifts to the poor and two gifts to friends. On Saturday the blessing: ". . . Who wroughtest miracles . . ." is to be intoned, the *parashah wayyabo 'Amalek* and the prophetical lesson to *pekude* are to be chanted, presents to be sent and the festival of Purim is to be discussed at length. Sunday sees dressing up in Sabbath clothes, visiting, the festival meal and the sending of portions.

Today in the diaspora the order of the Purim service is simple. In many communities the *Megillah* is read on the Saturday nights of Adar till the fourteenth. If one has forgotten to read the book of Esther on the night of the thirteenth, the offence is not serious, as the duty of read-

ing Esther may be fulfilled on the fourteenth. As Benjamin is careful to explain,
the book must be read from a scroll of
vellum or parchment, though nowadays
if there are present less than a *minyan* or
quorum of ten a printed text may be used.
The reader must stand while chanting
Esther. The prayers are the same as those
on other days of gratitude for miracles
except that *Hallel* is not read since the
Megillah takes its place. It will be remembered that the *Sefer Torah* is taken out
of the ark and three *parashot* read from
wayyabo 'Amalek (Ex. 17).

Of Purim customs the most ancient and
the most widespread is that founded on
the interpretation of the two verses: "Thou
shalt wipe out the memory of Amalek"
(Deut. 25.19) and "The name of the wicked
shall rot" (Prov. 10.7). Abudarham
relates that in his time the children used
to make wooden and stone effigies of
Haman, and write his name upon them;
and that whenever the name was mentioned
during the reading of the *Megillah* they

would smite their effigies lustily. Buxtorf in his *Synagoga Judaica* speaks of the shouting and banging in the synagogue at the mention of Haman's name. In his *Riti Hebraici*, written perhaps as a Jewish counterpart to Buxtorf's work, Leon of Modena gives an account of the rites and customs of contemporary, that is, sixteenth century, Jewry. He says that "While this book (Esther) is being read, there are some that, as often as they hear Haman named, they beat the ground, and make a great murmuring noise in token of cursing him and execrating his memorie; and they do the like at their morning prayers also." (Chilmead's translation.) There are certain familiar pictures of the Dutch synagogue in the seventeenth century which portray the Purim service. Two of the more youthful members of the congregation, adorned with three-cornered hats and large prayer shawls, are seen in a corner smiting a stone on which the name of Haman has been written. In Eastern Europe it was even a custom to write the name of Haman

on the soles of one's shoes and to rub out
the name in the dust of the floor. A visitor
to the Sephardi Synagogue in London in
the early nineteenth century describes
how the immigrants from Poland who sat
meekly on the back benches were wont
to write the name of Haman on a slip of
paper and industriously to erase it with
india rubber during the reading of the
Megillah. The more orthodox in the community of Aden to this day preserve a
form of this custom.[37] After the service,
when the head of the house returns home,
he takes paper and writes Haman's name
on it in ink, then proceeds to wash it off
in a cup of water. It is worthy of note
that the Jerusalem Talmud records what
may have been the precedent of this custom. It is said that when Esther 2.6 was
read, the men of Jerusalem would cry out:
"Nebuchadnezzar, may his bones be
crushed!" Today the children make a
loud noise with rattles, *grager* (Polish
grzegarz) or *Haman klappers* and stamp
every time the names of Haman and his

ten sons are mentioned. The burning of
an effigy of Haman, a custom which prevailed anciently in Israel, fell early, except
in the East, into desuetude.

In talmudic and Gaonic times Haman
was burnt in effigy and the young men
danced gleefully around the bonfire. The
text which affords the evidence[38] admits
of two renderings; either that the men
danced round or that they swung over the
fire. In Persia today the children set up
a beam of wood or iron in a courtyard,
hang the effigy of Haman on to it, pour
oil on the effigy and dance round it while
it burns, shouting "Haman! Haman! The
wicked Haman!" This eastern custom
seems to corroborate Ginzberg's explanation that it was the effigy which was hung
up on a ring, and to contradict Davidson's
rendering which implies that the young
men swung themselves over the fire by
the aid of a ring hung on the gallows.
Al-Beruni,[39] the celebrated Arabian geographer, in his book on the Jews tells how
Purim was celebrated in the tenth century

in Persia. "The feast of Purim," he says, "is called the feast of the Megillah and also *Haman-ṣur* (images of Haman); for on this day they make figures which they beat and then burn, imitating the burning (sic!) of Haman on the fourteenth and fifteenth of Adar." The conception which lies behind the burning of Haman in effigy is the general belief among the more primitive peoples in sympathetic magic. Rabbi Eleazar of Worms of the fourteenth century is intrigued by the magic rites practiced in his age. In his work entitled *The Book of Angels*, in speaking of magic, he describes rites closely parallel with this Purim custom. "It doth seem to me," says Rabbi Eleazar, "that the witches prepare for themselves likenesses in wax named after the man (whom they desire to persecute), and that whatever harm they may do to the image will befall that man." He continues with an account of a similar practice wherein an image is made by the witch on a wall to bring mishap at her behest on the person whom it represents. It appears from Schudt's *Jüdische Merkwürdigkeiten* that in later medieval times wax images of Haman and his ten sons were brought into the synagogue at Frankfort and were lit when they began to read the *Megillah*. This custom was forbidden by the Christians who, imagining the image of Haman on the gallows to be that of Christ, condemned the ceremony as one of mockery.

Kalonymos ben Kalonymos tells that in the fourteenth century the Jews used to celebrate the downfall of Haman by riding through the streets on horseback holding palm branches, and that they made merry round a puppet of Haman set up on high, uttering shouts of vengeance and blowing trumpets. This was known as *Ira*, the Italian for revenge. Chorny records that the burning of Haman in effigy is still (1884) common among the Jews of Kutais (Caucasia), except that it is not done publicly. He says that on Purim the wife prepares a piece of black wood in the kitchen by the fire against her

husband's return from synagogue. No
sooner has he entered than he asks his
wife what the piece of black wood is. She
replies, "It is Haman!" whereupon he
screams and shouts that it be forthwith
burned. They both kick the wood and
throw it into the fire. To this day Haman
is burnt annually in effigy in Jerusalem
and in Persia.

In order to give the book of Esther the
appearance of a letter it was a custom in
Israel to unroll it entirely on the reader's
desk.

In the fourteenth century the book of
Esther was read in the synagogue in
Spanish for the pleasure of the women,[40]
which is paralleled in Persia today where
the story is lengthily expounded in Persian.
Megillah 18a allows the reading of Esther
in any language intelligible to the community, but Soferim 21 demands that it
be read in Hebrew. When the rigorous
pietist Isaac ben Sheshet found that the
community at Saragossa, whither he had
come to take up offlce as Rabbi of the

congregation, was wont to read Esther in Spanish, he was deeply shocked. The local Rabbis were far more complacent than himself; and so with the aid of Nissim Gerundi he set about to eradicate this custom which had been in force at Saragossa for some thirty years. The ground of objection is described by Graetz as "sophistical"; it is certainly very strange. The two learned men argued that as the reader understood Hebrew it was not lawful for him to read the scroll of Esther in any other language, though the women who did not understand Hebrew might lawfully hear the book read in Spanish. Another argument was more weighty. As had been done some thousand years earlier with the Septuagint, so now with the Spanish text, Rabbi Isaac questioned the accuracy of the rendering, on which count he was able to enforce the reading in Hebrew. It is worthy of note that the vernacular seems to have been more used in the medieval synagogue than in the modern one, and that this was in accordance with Jewish feeling which had anciently approved of the rendering of the Bible into Aramaic when this language had become the common speech of Israel.

Addresses calling on the men in the synagogue to make merry are not uncommon in the various liturgies. In the Roman, Venetian and Bologna services Abraham ibn Ezra's *piyyut*[41] is recited after the reading of the *Megillah* in which the following lines occur. "Set up in faithful testimony these events and miracles, while in thy mouth set honey and manna, the story of Haman. Go, eat dainties and drink deep of mead!" In the Spanish ritual on the Sabbath before Purim the congregation recites Judah Halevi's poem which begins: "Friends, come eat and drink till ye are drunk, fill Purim's days with joy!" In the Roman service some of the merrymaking occurred within the walls of the synagogue. The worshipers are directed to clap their hands, to stamp their feet on the ground and, to increase the din, to hurl earthenware vessels on the floor.

Nor is this rejoicing in the synagogue peculiar to the Jews of the West. In Jerusalem on the eve of Purim, just before night rushes down, one may see the Sephardim in their Sabbath best, wending their way to synagogue.[42] Each man, dressed in a long robe and wide-brimmed hat, holds in his hand the present he received on his betrothal: a *Megillah* in a case carved wondrously in wood or delicately in silver. Soon they reach the synagogue, now lit up with all manner of lights in honor of Purim, where before the afternoon service each man gives the equivalent of the ancient half shekel in memory of the Temple charity: in Turkish times half a *mejidi*, today ten piasters. These coins are either distributed to the poor on the next day or put aside for some special purpose. When the afternoon prayers have been duly said and the customary blessings chanted, the reading of the *Megillah* begins. Scarcely has the reader come to the words, "Haman this wicked man," before the whole congregation is indulging in such an orgy of stamping and shouting that the voice of the reader can no longer be heard. When the tumult dies down, the reader repeats the phrase and continues with his task. Though recently the children have taken to providing themselves with *gragers* from the Ashkenazi hucksters in Jerusalem, the "rattling" of Haman is not a genuine Sephardi custom. Almost too soon, the reading is over, and the ultimate blessing has been said; the congregation proceeds to pass a vote of censure on Haman, Zeresh and their brood, by stamping and kicking so violently that their clamor becomes overwhelming. Slowly the noise dies down and the congregation goes home to tell those who have been unable to be present at the service the wonderful story of Esther and then to join in the happy festival meal.

In the Yemenite community at Aden, whose origin is still so dubious, it is regarded as a great privilege to read the *Megillah* to the congregation; a privilege which is bought by a gift of oil and wax

to light up the synagogue.[43] Three years
ago, when electric light was installed, the
gift was commuted to one of money. Here
the newly wedded grooms vie one with
another for the honor of reading the
Megillah. It so happened that on one
occasion several bridegrooms in Aden
quarreled among themselves, each desiring
to bring the necessary oil and wax. Unable
to solve their dispute, they brought it
before the *Bet Din* (court of justice). The
problem was solved simply; the privilege
was put for public auction and the highest
bidder given the right to provide light for
the service and to read the *Megillah*.

Before these Sephardim of Arabia read
the scroll of Esther, it is a tradition among
them to recite certain verses extolling the
miracles and mercies of God, as for instance,
"I shall make mention of the loving-kind-
ness of God."   After these prefatory
invocations the *hazzan* (reader) cries out,
"Blessed be so and so, the bridegroom."
He who has been named stands up, takes
the scroll of Esther in his hands, opens it,

and says: "With your permission, gentle-
men!", to which all reply: "With the
permission of Heaven!" He then pronounces the benediction and proceeds to
chant each verse in two divisions; the first
half is whispered after him by the congregation, while the second they recite in a
loud voice together. When he has read
half way through the *Megillah*, a second
bridegroom, who on the following morning
will read the first half of the *Megillah*, is
called up to read the second half. Noteworthy is the lighting of ten candles both
at the evening and at the morning services; a relic, no doubt, of the similar
custom of burning ten wax images recorded
of medieval observance in Frankfort.

In Persia, some weeks before the festival,
the children pass many hours daily in
writing out the book of Esther in the
square script, which when completed they
take to synagogue on the great day.[44]
Already on *Shabbat Zakor*, the *mulla* or
interpreter by reading the *Tikkun Purim*
between the morning and the *musaf* ser-

vices, prepares his congregation for the festival. Then he reads the Torah, and as soon as he comes to the words: "Thou shalt blot out the memory of Amalek from under the heavens; Thou shalt not forget," the whole congregation begins to hammer with their fists on the desks and tables and also to stamp on the floor. Afternoon sees them once more assembled in the synagogue to hear the *tafsir* or the explanation of Esther in Persian from the *Targum Sheni*. More especially is that synagogue patronized where the *mulla* knows how to ornament his discourse with stories, legends and similes from daily experience which go straight to the heart. The women too throng to their section of the synagogue to hear these strange and marvelous tales. As vividly as if he saw them enacted before him, the *mulla* describes the enchanting legends which are to be found in the *Targum Sheni*. The congregation are all ears, they sit closely attentive, they drink in his words, and live through every incident of the story he recounts. When

Israel is harassed the whole assembly groans and sighs as one man, but as soon as their lot improves all rejoice and cry out Bah! Bah! (a cry of joy). When the *mulla* tells them how completely Haman was discomfited, the eyes of every member of the congregation light up with joy; they curse Haman and his following; they are happy that Israel has overcome the enemy; and they leave the synagogue, though fatigued both by their lesson and by the emotions which their ready sympathy has evoked, yet happy and spiritually strengthened by the issue of the story.

For the Persian Jew the fast of Esther is as binding as that on the Day of Atonement. Even those who are ill take it upon themselves to make the law more strict than it is and refuse to touch the food which their relatives press on them, while the children of eight, nine and ten run away from their parents so that they shall not be forced to eat. The older children are wont on this day to exert their authority upon their younger brothers and sisters, by catching them when they run away and stuffing food into their mouths. The fast over, the entire Jewish congregation gathers together either in private houses or in the synagogues. The streets of the Jewish quarter are void of any wayfarer but silence does not reign; the children have bought for themselves *trake* and *pishpishak*, squibs and bombs, and sparks, flying everywhere, accompany the reverberating crashes of the fireworks. Before the evening prayer the *gabbay* (treasurer of the congregation), according to a custom in force in some parts of Persia, takes a copper tray on which he has put two shekels and goes the round of the congregation. As he stops to rattle his tray before each man he is given a donation of some small change. The money so gathered is used either for synagogue purposes or is sent to the fund of Rabbi Meir Ba'al ha-Nes, i. e. to the poor of Jerusalem.

Each synagogue has among its treasures a parchment scroll of the *Megillah* from which the representative of the congregation reads, while the *mulla* and his companions follow in the same text. The rest of the community, in view of their ignorance, listen to the recital without any text before them. The service has begun, the blessings have been chanted, the book of Esther is being read while the murmur of the children who are following the reader *viva voce* increases; all ears strain tensely in anticipation of the first mention of Haman. Scarcely has the reader finished the verse! "After these things the king Ahasuerus raised up Haman son of Hammedatha the Agagite," than a frenzy of noise breaks forth; the fireworks are let off; fists smite the desks and the walls, feet drum on the floor till the building rings again with the din. The children can no longer be controlled. Those who desire to fulfill their religious obligations can only close in with the fast growing crowd round the reader. Meanwhile the thunder of the children continues increasing and deafening; one casts violently explosive bombs which go off on impact; another

screams to his heart's content; another
whistles spasmodically, shouting in the
intervals; another kicks every piece of
furniture he can lay feet on, until most
of the congregation are dazed with noise.
The tumult continues shattering and
uproarious long after the reading is over,
till every child has had his fill of shouting
and knows the joy of a long desired aim
attained. In most synagogues both after
the evening reading of the *Megillah* and
after the morning reading *Halwa Koshke* or
Turkish delight is given to the celebrants.

In Hamadan, near the traditional tomb
of Esther and Mordecai, the Jews gather
to hold the Purim service. In the narrow
space by the tombstones they read the
Megillah and stay on after to study the
Talmud. It is general in Persia for a family
which has recently been bereaved of one
of its members to stay at home on the
days of Purim and to invite ten men to
hold the service there, who will also say
a prayer for the repose of the soul of the
departed.

In the seventeenth century Holland was the center of Hebrew studies for the Christian scholars in Europe. On April 20, 1653, in Utrecht, the far-famed Johannes Leusden disputes with his pupils before he can confer on them the title of doctor. It is the thesis of one of his pupils which gives an account of the *Megillah*. Henricus van Rhenen, already a pastor of the church, is being examined on the book of Esther. Dr. Leusden asks: "Why was the queen called Esther?" Henricus, no doubt very well prepared, replies in sonorous Latin that the Jews hold that Esther was so called because of her nature, *mesatteret* (hiding), since she hid her words and concealed her origin. Others maintain that her name was given her because she was called Venus which is *Istahar* in Aramaic and not unrelated to the word *aster* in Greek. Among the other books of the Bible this book is commonly called *Megillat Ester* or the *volumen Estherae*. The word *Megillah* is derived from the root *galal*, "to roll", because the ancient

Jews were accustomed to write out the
book of Esther on one continuous piece
of skin. The Jews of to-day still imitate
their forefathers. But Dr. Leusden, want-
ing further details, promptly questions his
pupil; "In what manner, then, were they
accustomed to write their manuscript?"
Henricus van Rhenen replies that the
Jews are accustomed to write out the book
of Esther as they write the Pentateuch, on
a continuous skin rolled round a spindle
of wood. Some scrolls, he finds, are written
without vowels or other accents and some
even without marking off the verses or
chapters.   He, Henricus van Rhenen,
possesses two such copies of Esther written
on a continuous skin, of which one is a
foot, and the other nearly three feet wide,
but both alike destitute of vowels or
accents, and the division of verse or chapter.   Henricus now feels rather more at
home with his subject and gives a long
disquisition on the κεραία or *cornicula*
(tittles) with which certain of the letters
are adorned.   He does not, however,

mention the fact that many scribes, in order to make up for the absence of the name of God, write its constituent letters larger whenever they occur fairly close together; so that the reader sees the holy name emerge, as it were, out of the text.

There are a number of prescriptions with which one must comply in writing out any part of the Bible for liturgical use. The parchment must be prepared from the skin of a clean animal, usually a sheep or a goat, and is in itself to be kept ritually pure. It is to be sewn into a scroll only with clean animal's sinews. Lines are not ruled but are pressed for the guidance of the scribe, into the parchment. Tradition dictates the exact number of words per line, and the exact number of lines per column, while all lines must begin and end underneath one another. The ink is to be made fresh by the scribe himself according to a known recipe, and while writing the scroll the scribe must keep himself ritually clean.

Most Jewish families possess copies

of the *Megillah* which they put aside in a leather case against the festival. Naturally those scrolls in the possession of the richer families are more lavishly ornamented, and many have cases exquisitely carved both in silver and in gold; they are fine examples of native Jewish art. Among most manuscript collections are to be found a number of *Megillot Ester*. The workmanship of their cases as well as the delicacy of their lettering often commands admiration. The earlier *Megillot*, more especially those written in Italy in the fourteenth and fifteenth centuries, seem to carry on that high standard of perfection for which their Christian models are so justly famed. Even earlier, in the manuscripts which were written in France and Germany, the style of the illuminations as of the pictures with which a scribe like Benjamin of France decorated his work, shows that the technique had been learnt either from the clerks or from the professional illuminators. It may be true to say that the vogue of ornamenting the first letters of the chapters began in southern France and western Germany in the twelfth and thirteenth centuries and then traveled to Italy in the late fourteenth and early fifteenth centuries, where it received encouragement from the prevailing modes of illumination. When Jewry made its way to Eastern Europe the ornate manner of writing *Megillot* seems to have been dropped in favor of ingeniously constructed cases of chased silver and other metal work.

The size varies over a fairly wide range, the smallest being written in letters so minute that they are barely legible, while the largest are the same as the standard *Sefer Torah*, or scroll of the Law which is used in the ordinary service.

CHAPTER III.

"*Ibi tunc (after reading the Megillah) nulla superest exsilii memoria, gaudent omnes, jubilant, exsultant, mirosque Hamani triumphos agunt.*"

(*Thereafter abideth no memory of the Exile; all men rejoice, make merry, exult, and enact the wondrous triumph over Haman*).

WILLIAM SCHICKARD IN HIS
SPEECH ON PURIM AT TÜBIN-
GEN ON FEBRUARY 14, 1634.

CHAPTER III

THE CELEBRATION IN THE HOME

The ultimate unit of Jewry is the home. More particularly is this true of medieval and ghetto days when this Holy of Holies, by uniting the individual members of the family, was able to keep alive the corporate spirit of the race. It is no wonder, then, that in the home where there are observed the feasting and the giving of portions, both integral parts of the festival, the days of Purim are days of gladness.

Nor is the banquet only one of food; as the learned Steinschneider has observed,[45] it is a *mishteh*, drink the primary consideration and eating merely incidental. Even the Talmud proclaims[46] that at the festival meal one should drink till he cannot distinguish between *'arur Haman* (cursed be Haman!) and *baruk Mordekai* (blessed be Mordecai). The distinction is a subtle one: both phrases by *Gematria*, that is by counting up the numerical value of the letters, are equal to five hundred and two and in *Gematria* as in Geometry the axiom holds true that things which are equal to the same thing are equal to each other. In spite of certain Rabbis who explain the Talmud maxim as hyperbole, who say that the distinction is lost in the sleep which even a moderate drink would induce, the Jewish proverb still describes a man of unusual sobriety as "Drunk the whole year round and sober on Purim."

The sending of presents, in Yiddish *shalachmones* from the Hebrew *mishloah manot*, is aptly arranged: the poor man sends his rich neighbor an inexpensive dainty, often a humble orange, and receives in return a heap of rich dishes or the money with which to buy them. In medieval days the practice of making gifts extended to Christian servants as well.[47] When there is a lack of rich men, as in Aden and parts of Eastern Europe today, whole families which are neither poor enough to be fed at the expense of the community

nor rich enough to buy one another presents, acquit themselves of their duty by
exchanging suppers. It has been known
for a Purim gift to be the dedication of a
book.

Purim is also a festival of charity. When
the Temple stood each worshiper gave his
mahazit ha-shekel or half-shekel to the
poor.[48] The Talmud in speaking of *magbit
Purim* and of *ma'ot Purim* (Purim money)
refers to additional contributions to charity
which though not obligatory were general.
It is known moreover that the Roman
administrators of Judea in the first century
of this era gave the Jews persmission to
collect certain funds for the needs of the
community. Friday was the regular day
for this grant of aid to the poor,[49] while
meals were given free at all times in the
soup kitchens.[50] On Purim special collections were made for dowering unprovided
brides and for ransoming Jewish captives.
In early rabbinic times a collection was
regularly made to provide the needy with
Purim meals and for no other purpose;

since it is said "Purim collections are exclusively for Purim."[51] Among the laws of the Jewish community in the Comtat Venaissin (i. e. Avignon) in the sixteenth and seventeenth centuries, mention is made of the charity distributed on Purim.[52] Articles LXVII and LXXXVI speak of the gifts imposed on young married couples, the distribution of victuals and the banquet at the community's expense on the day of the festival of "Purym." In London at the beginning of the nineteenth century the *Purim gelt*, so an eyewitness records, was given by the *Zedoko gabbay*,[53] who was wont to thrust a shilling through the gate of the synagogue in Duke's Place and allow the strongest beggar to fight through the crowd for the coin. According to Joseph Ometz the Persian Jews are not alone in their custom of sending the *mahazit ha-shekel* to the poor of Jerusalem. This support of the *halukkah* is known to many even today as the charity of Rabbi Meir Ba'al ha-Nes. In every Jewish congreg ation Purim is the day when no beggar may be refused, and when gifts are forced on those for whom recent misfortune makes it hard to beg. As a special gift the *ma'ot Purim* or Purim money was often sent to the Rabbi and the teachers. Purim in any Jewish quarter sees the children, ever proud of their privilege, running in the streets, holding a parcel tightly to their bosoms, anxious to reach their destination without mishap, where after delivering the Purim gift and taking another in exchange, some sweet morsel will surely be given them.

"Whosoever does work on Purim," says the proverb, "shall never see the sign of a blessing." But on the day before this festival every Jewish household seethes with activity: cooking must be done both for the banquet and for a day's meals. The popular dishes throughout the ages are almost without number. According to the *Hymn for the night of Purim*,[54] the thirteenth century Jews of Provence preferred above all things geese and chickens and used to avoid the staple crushed lentils. In his tractate on Purim, the famous *Masseket Purim*,[55] Kalonymos ben Kalonymos, an Italian Jewish poet and scholar of the fifteenth century, tells of the *maakalim* (delicacies) which the Italian Jews then prepared for Purim. He says, parodying the style of the Talmud:— "Rabbi Mordecai said: Twenty-four dishes were told to Moses on Mount Sinai all of which a man must prepare on Purim. They are i. *kesami* (*fritere chose e gustose collaradice odoratissimo del casto*); ii. *molaytot* (Pes. 74a); iii. *tortoli* (*torticcine*); iv. rusks; v. *tortoliche* (*torte*); vi. *mostazzoli* (*mosstacuioli* = pastries); vii. *tocchato* (*toccheto* or ragout); viii. pouches (Ket. 17b); ix. *itinyan* (*tocanie colla inferno*); x. hart's flesh; xi. venison; xii. flesh of the fallow buck; xiii. geese; xiv. chickens; xv. pigeons; xvi. and xvii. the flesh of young birds and fowls; xviii. swans; xix. *anatre* (ducks); xx. *fasani* (pheasants); xxi. *perdicci* (*pernici*, partridges); xxii. *folacche* (*folage*, young turkeys or moor hens); xxiii. *kaluyvini* (*culaccio*, paunch of stuffed fowl); xxiv. *kotornicii* (*colornici*, quails). We learn that in addition to these dishes are prescribed pancakes, maccaroni and jellies."

A poem for the festival in Italian and Hebrew which reached its second edition in Venice in 1700 would indicate that Jewish cookery continued to be so richly varied. The first part contains a list of dishes for *un Gran Banchetto* which is admittedly imposing.

"Salted chickens' necks and fat cakes, huge pigeons and partridges and pheasants and quails to continue the abandon of the day; fruits and fine preserves of every season, every clime, preserves in alcohol, of many colors and much joy."

The Hebrew section begins with a verse which speaks of the proverbial sweet tooth of the Sephardim. "Bring ye quickly sweets and fruits, and like the Sephardim place them on the banquet table."

About 1800 London had imported from Eastern Europe certain Purim cakes.[56] From Duke's Place to Goulston Street in Whitechapel a vast Purim fair was held where the masqueraders took the law into their own hands and the hawkers sold *gingerle* (gingerbread) and *malina* pies (raspberry pies). In western Jewry today the festival is marked by three special dishes: the first is *Kreplach*, or *Kreppchen*, *Hamanöhren*, or *orecchi di Aman* (small dough pouches containing chopped meat) which are eaten, it appears, only on those days when there is beating and banging; thus, on the eve of the day of Atonement, because of the *makkot* or thirty-nine stripes (not forty in view of the interpretation of Deut. 25.3:—"Forty stripes he may give him, he shall not exceed; lest, if he should exceed, and beat him above these with many stripes, then thy brother should seem vile to thee."); on *Hosha'na Rabbah* because of the beating of the willow; and on Purim, because of the beating when Haman's name is mentioned. In memory of Ahasuerus who ruled from Ethiopia unto India, the extremely orthodox among Jewry eat the *tarnegol hodu* (cock of India,

a literal translation of the Russian name)
or Turkey.   Far more general are the
babbelech, *bab*, or salted beans boiled in
their jackets which are eaten, so we are
told, in memory of Daniel's diet of cereals.
The standard cakes called *Haman-taschen*,
from *man* (Yiddish), poppy-seed (from the
Hebrew word for manna) and *taschen*
pouches, are shaped like a three-cornered
hat and filled with poppy seeds well mixed
with honey. This mixture is first mentioned
by Abraham ibn Ezra (1092–1167) as a
sweet-meat for Purim.[57]

In the matter of drink wine was of course
always popular. Provençal Jews seem to
have favored white and red wines and
a certain green wine, by which a liqueur
may well be meant.[58] Italy in the fifteenth
century produced a special Purim brew
of honey and wine called *oinomeli*.[59]   In
eastern Europe wine, mead and vodka or
brandy are the most popular drinks; beer
never seems to have been liked by Jews.

In the quarter of the Sephardim in
Jerusalem Adar brings in its wake the

great season for the Jewish confectioners who show their resource in making out of sugar all sorts of images.[60] Their ingenuity knows no bounds; they make *megillot*, inkpots, pens, baskets, sandals, shoes, scales, scissors, clocks, chains, mirrors, cups, coins, nets, ladders, cots, books, the Messiah riding on a donkey, Elijah with a trumpet in his hand, Mordecai the righteous riding on a horse, Esther the queen, Haman hanging on his gallows, and the ten sons of Haman. Even the Arabs have noticed their Jewish neighbors treating themselves with a generous superflux of sweetmeats on this day and call Purim the "festival of sugar,"[61] much in the same way as they call the Day of Atonement the "festival of the chicken" on account of the chicken slaughtered publicly for a *kapparah* (Atonement) on the eve of this fast day.

The festival meal is here a royal banquet, where all the celebrants eat, drink, sing, make merry and distribute copper coins to the delighted children. Early on the morning of the day of Purim one may see the Sephardim hurrying to the synagogue to get the morning service over quickly. Soon the beggars, even more shameless than at other times, will stop everyone and ask for charity; the beggars have waited a whole year for this day. When the morning service is over the men return home and, having read the *Megillah* to the women-folk, they begin to eat the cakes and pastries and drink a little *arak*. Their fast broken, they distribute gifts to the members of the household, the nature of which is more determined by expediency than by custom.

Apart from the regular mendicants who go from door to door, there are the incidental visitors who request of the house-owner's goodwill a little charity in return for a thousand thousand blessings. It is the duty of the head of the house to satisfy the wants of every poor man who comes his way; a task which is never easy. The *shammash*, the *gabbay*, and the grave-diggers join in the throng of widows and orphans and men of importance who take it upon themselves to make collections for families in distress. The day is indeed an auspicious one for charity. But there is no end. Even non-Jewish beggars come to join in the *mizvah* (good deed) of accepting charity. They are followed by Jewish singers and players with timbrels, violins, lutes, flutes and cymbals, who ask charity for their music. Some come masked, others masquerade in fancy dress richly brocaded in gold.

The chief sexton presents himself at the house of a prosperous merchant, wearing a red turban in towering folds upon his head, his garments decorated with almond leaves, and with such flowers as are in season and sweet smelling spices. The children are delighted with their entertainer whom they load with fresh cakes and sweets. In return he sings the *conflas*, so popular a ballad that every singer takes it upon himself to modify and improve both the text and the melody. There follows a selection, partly phonetic and partly in Spanish, from one of the versions of this Judeo-Spanish song known in Jerusalem to-day.[62]

"*Haman* se emborracho y salio azwaire (a los aires?) a los hijos (or niños) demando que *parsha* ire (hara). Dijieron '*wa'era, wa'era el abhram,*' y que tenemos un padre rahman que nos efayada y a Haman le mate. Vive yo! Vive Esther! Vivan todos los Judios!

Empesar quiero contar ayudas del dio alto de lo que quiero enmentar nada yo no falta, con bailes y saltos y con gran placer, porque Haman *almamzer* nos quiso matarnos tambien atimarnos."

This might be rendered:— "Haman got drunk and went out into the street and asked the children what *parashah* it was. They replied: 'wa'era, wa'era el Abram.' What a merciful God is our Father who has mercy on us but who slays Haman. Long may I live! Long live Queen Esther! Long live all the Jews!

"And now I begin to tell and to relate the works of God on high, such of them as I remember, none shall be lacking. With leaping, with dancing and with great pleasure shall I sing how Haman the bastard sought to slay us and to break us."

While the children are being entertained by the song the mother is extremely busy arranging the gifts. She honors relations with some rare dish cooked by her own hands and sends her friends delicacies bought in the market. Each one receives an appropriate gift, the sons getting in sugar *megillah*, pen, inkstand, watch, "a bride," scales, a ladder or any other symbol to remind them that when they reach man's estate their brides will send them these as gifts. An unmarried daughter receives in the same spirit a mirror, scissors, a basket, a baby's cot and "bridegroom's shoes" made of sugar. The real bridegroom sends his bride a tray covered with pieces of *pastaryl* (*pastaleria*, i. e. pastry) in the midst of which is a sugar hand, a *khamsa* (five fingers) or *Fatma* (named after the wife of Mohammed) to ward off the evil

eye. There also is placed some jewel set
in gold dedicated to the bride; this too is
guarded from the evil eye by a sprig of
rue. Some bridegrooms send with their
gift a dancing woman with tambourine.
No sooner have the feet of the messenger
touched the threshold of the bride's abode
than the dancing woman begins to play
the tambourine and, as she smites it, to
sing. The music is too tempting and the
whole of the bride's household, including
also the bride herself, begin to dance.
Should it happen that the bride's relatives
are men of established position, the bridegroom sends them presents as well, accompanied by a singing woman.

The bride's present to the groom is
determined by custom. A tray is laden
with *pastaryl* and a *Megillah* in a silver
case; a scribe's silver inkpot or a scribe's
silver chain, or a silver spice box reposes
in the midst of the pastry. Both bride and
bridegroom know what they will get since
the Purim gifts are stipulated in the
Tenaim, the marriage agreement.

The great *minhah* service which is held
in the afternoon serves as a prelude to the
feast. Many neighbors and friends find it
convenient to gather together for the
banquet for which one brings a jug of
brandy, another a barrel of wine together
with fine foods and rich pastries. All eat
their fill and drink more than sobriety
dictates. Songs follow on the meal; the
Jews of Babylon sing in Hebrew and in
Aramaic, a language which still prepon-
derates in their liturgy, those of Syria and
Egypt in Arabic and Hebrew, while the
Sephardim sing in Hebrew and Ladino.
The enthusiastic singing continues until
a peak of joy is reached when one of the
party rises attired in strange clothes. He
wears a huge turban, a fur put on back to
front; against his chest he carries a broom
as though it were a pike, standing before
the company a very sergeant of joy. He
takes up his parable in Ladino to tell of
Zeresh, Haman and the filthy garments
of their daughter. His speech is in rhymed
prose and this is the burden of his tale!

"May every sickness and every ill and every plague of Egypt, in fire and in water, in earth as in heaven, every smiting and affliction, loosening and baldness, foreheads without hair, blasting and cholera, destruction and scab, a predestined end, family shame, wrath and anger, noise in the morning and thunder at noonday, ire and overflowing wrath when three foregather over food, the discredit of angels and faithful ones rest upon a forgotten and faithless family for whom the place of burning is prepared. May disease be poured forth and emptied upon the head of Haman, whose hope is turned to death." Thus they amuse themselves invoking with glib lips a torrent of evil on Haman, looking all the while upon him who can drink most as the hero of the hour. The wine flows in streams, bottle after bottle of brandy is turned up to pour the last of its rich flow into the waiting throats. By the time the wine is drunk no one is sober and the maidens enter to dance before

an audience which sleeps and wakes and
sleeps again.

On this day the luxury, the ease and
the memory of miracles conspire to make
the Sephardi completely oblivious of the
bitterness and oppression of exile and to
induce in him utter happiness.

In Persia as in Jerusalem, the fortnight
before Purim sees the shops in the Jewish
quarters take on a new appearance.[63] The
floor of the shops which serves as a show
window is decorated with all manner of
sweetmeats and foods cooked specially for
Purim. The spirit of Purim reigns everywhere. In the schools they teach the book
of Esther, the *Tikkun Purim*, a code for
the observance of Purim, and suitable
piyyutim or religious poems. From every
house are heard snatches of Purim folk-
tunes which all sing as they go about their
congenial preparations. In a general way
no Persian Jew, and no Moroccan Jew,
bakes at home, but is in the habit of using
the local baker; on Purim however, he
usually hires a baker to cook in the house

and produce sweet wafers, long rusks, rice cakes, almond cakes and cakes of ground pistachio nuts.

In the richer classes the older children are writing out copies of the *Megillah*, the poorer and all the younger children are busy with an effigy of Haman. One sews the hands, another the feet, another the head, and another the trunk. When the cases are ready they fill them with straw, stubble and rags, and sew the constituent limbs together into a full-sized effigy of Haman.

After the service on the first evening of Purim the children remember only that "the city of Susa was exultant and joyful." Bands of them dress themselves up in all sorts of colored garments, paint their faces in many colors, chiefly black, and rush about from house to house, beating timbrels, leaping, dancing, shouting and singing. On account of the demands which the fast makes on the energy of most of the congregation, the Jews of Persia do not hold feasts on the first evening except

in Shiraz, Bulugird and some other towns,
where it is a custom to get up in the middle of the night, for then "the sleep of the
king was disturbed." They feast till daybreak and pass the night in drinking,
merrymaking and visiting friends. But
normally the silence of the Jewish quarters
till noon the next day is broken only by
the footfall of an occasional messenger.
Here, as in Jerusalem and Morocco,
custom demands that the betrothed send
gifts one to another. The groom arranges
a vast tray about a foot deep laden with
sweets, fruit, jewelry and golden ornaments
which he sends to his bride. Nor is it
only the bridegroom who sends a tray so
loaded to the bride; all who know her send
her loads of gifts in the measure of their
means, the nearness of their relationship
and warmness of their affection. At the
bride's house all her relatives and friends
foregather to receive the gifts and to feast
the festival.

The *se'udah* is held on the second night
of Purim either at the house of a newly

wedded couple or often enough in the
house of a man who likes *kif*, who likes
to pass much time in congenial company
chatting and cracking jokes. Once they
are assembled, the gathering behaves for
a while with fully Persian propriety, and
then slowly the company warms up. One
tells a joke and another caps it. The trays
and tables are laden with vegetables, in
Persia a luxury, various fruits, all sorts of
preserves, morsels of toasted food or *meze*
to accompany the drinking of the numerous bottles of wine and strong drink. Each
man, as the law requires, presses wine on
his fellow and continues to refill the goblet
which he holds in his hand. If by chance
one of the visitors is given a slightly smaller
glass than the others, he is apt to turn
upon his host and say: "Would you give
a camel water out of the palm of your
hand?" Wine induces good spirits, the
happy throng begins to sing in chorus and
the harmony swells till all burn with joy
and sweat with song. They know well how
to cast opprobrium on Haman. They sing

taunting ballads out of the *Esther-nameh*,
the epic of Esther modeled at least in
form on Firdawsi's *Shah-nameh*. Perhaps
better known than any other part of this
poem is the section which tells how Vashti
was invited by the King to his banquet
and the preparation for the hanging of
Haman.

Vashti replies to the King's invitation
in these words:—

"And Vashti answered the king and
said:—'So drunk art thou become, O
camel! that thine eyes cannot see, so how
can thy command stand in my regard?
Thou art become the chief stable-boy in
the stable, fit only to be saved by my
father!'"

The words which Ahasuerus spake unto
his officers: "Arrogance has this woman
shown to her king and to her husband.
I'll burn her or slay her with a blow of
the sword."

After Esther has asked of Ahasuerus at
the banquet that he deliver the Jews from
Haman the oppressor, Ahasuerus goes out

into his garden. There he sees angels who appear to him in the semblance of mortals, busily uprooting the trees. In his wrath the king asks them what they are doing. They reply:—"From here we uproot to plant over there; in the garden of Haman shall we plant them." Naturally, Ahasuerus swears vengeance on his presumptuous minister. The story embellished by legend goes on to tell of the hanging of Haman and the prosperity of Israel. Thus the time passes in songs, dances, games and drinking till all are drunk and dawn breaks up the party.

During the days of Purim it is customary among the Persian Jews to gamble at a game called *kimar*. Another diversion is *kab* in which the bones of the sheep's knee-joint are used as dice on the fall of which the players stake their money. It would appear that this game is too exciting and that most refrain from playing it all the year round and content themselves with the game of *kab* on Purim. In *takti-ner* a board is divided into two sections, in

each of which black and white wooden
counters are arranged in fixed order. The
winner is he who throws two of his men
into two small compartments in his oppo-
nent's section. Of card games *gangafe* is
most widely played, but chess in spite of
its reputed origin in Persia is not known.

No Purim evening is well passed without gambling of some sort, which was
practiced not so much for material gain
as to give excitement, to gratify vanity
and to vindicate prowess.[64] That gambling
is almost an innovation in Jewry is seen
first, because the ancient Hebrews had
no knowledge of it, had in point of fact
no word to express this conception, and
second, since there is no attack on it till
the late fifteenth century. It is true that
Jacob Levi who lived at the end of the
fourteenth and the beginning of the fifteenth centuries gives an explanation of
the Talmud precept that the dice player
is not acceptable as a witness, but he does
not condemn. He says that this ruling
applies only to those who play with pledges

or for credit but when the stake is on the table there is no conditioned approval. Then he refers to the story told in the tractate Sabbath of the Talmud (fol. 30b) which tells how two men had a wager that the one if he could provoke Hillel to anger would take from the other the sum of four hundred *zuzim*. Hillel's patience is proverbial: the man lost his bet. The first of the Jewish moralists (who as a general rule leave no passion and no human weakness uncondemned) to launch an attack on betting is Moses ha-Cohen ben Eleazar who in 1473 denounced betting for pecuniary gain. In his book, *Sefer ha-Hasidim*, he refers to it by the German word *wetten*, philologically the same as the English "bet." Language condemns the *waghals* as a rash person.

A system of morals will perforce disapprove of gambling. It will readily be conceded that in most forms of gambling, whether skill plays the greater or the lesser part, it is accident on which victory most depends. Accident does not depend on any ethical laws nor does it intelligently choose between promoting human happiness and bringing about sorrow. Chance plays but a small part in the life of a religious man whose trust is entirely in his God. The inveterate gambler is usually a fatalist or a believer in strange and occult sciences which teach him how to woo Lady Fortune and how to get her favors. Thus it is that believing Jews who hold the lot of man to be a direct dispensation from God, cannot conscientiously hold with betting. It says much for the license of Purim that gambling in the evening is so popular and frowned upon so little.

Both the Persian and the Sephardi modes of celebration have, for the student of Jewish manners and customs, a peculiar importance. The names of the Sephardi dishes go back to a time before the expulsion from Spain. Just as their general behavior without doubt goes back to the early middle ages in Europe, so does the Persian celebration mirror today in certain of its aspects the rites of talmudic and gaonic Babylon. The Sephardi, who has been referred to as the sergeant of joy, and the poetic sexton are the licensed Purim entertainers whose portraits meet us in the post-Renaissance copper-plates with which accounts of Purim were illustrated. The broom is characteristic of the jester who used pots for bells and the saucepan for his cap.

The Talmud collection for dowering brides, the spirit of communism which ruled in medieval times,[65] the special charity which newly married couples gave in the Comtat Venaissin, the bridegrooms who read the *Megillah*, the exchange of gifts between bride and groom in Jerusalem, and the celebration at the house of the newly wedded in Persia; all these point to an undercurrent of tradition which sees fit to link with Purim the rejoicing of husband and wife, which establishes Purim's happy memories in the home by bringing the festival early to the notice of its founders.

CHAPTER IV.

"Heint iz Purim, morgen iz aus;
Gibt mir a dreier, und warft mich araus."

AN OLD VERSE.

CHAPTER IV

The Celebration Outside the Home

Sir Walter Scott in reviving an interest in the Middle Ages in England tended to substitute for squalid history a pageant of splendor. Though a little later the balance of truth was more than righted by the investigations of Maitland, yet there is more justification for this pageantry at certain periods than the tables of feudal statistics would admit; for it was out of these colorful aspects of medieval society, which the Romanticists painted more vividly than nature, that the Purim masquerade was born. The golden age of the troubadour saw the birth of this Purim child who, as a babe in arms, was rescued from the fierce French rioting and carried to Italy. There, the carnivals, despite the rough treatment they meted out to the child's parents, fostered and encouraged his playful habits and endowed him with that adolescent energy which maintained him till the time when, with features well defined, he was to travel as far afield as Russia in one direction and Palestine in the other.

The Purim king in Provence was a counterpart of the buffoon monarch of the Feast of Fools and was to become, by the seventeenth century, the Purim Rabbi. Nor is there much doubt that the masques of the popes played a part in the evolution of the Purim play which did not appear in an articulated dramatic shape until the eighteenth century in Germany.

Purim celebrations were to manifest themselves in widely differing forms and to absorb a long series of embellishments, national and local, before their culmination in the nineteenth century masquerade in Eastern Europe and the twentieth century revival in Tel Aviv. Let us examine this complicated evolution in greater detail.

The opulence of the imperial administration of Rome persisted in early medieval times in south-eastern France, where a shadow of the earlier Roman constitution had survived. French Jewry came under this Roman influence and in appointing for itself both kings and consuls their action was due partly to the Roman model and partly to that desire for autonomy which Dubnow believes to be the keynote of Jewish history.

Languedoc and Provence prospered from the twelfth till the thirteenth centuries. The yoke of the distant kings of France and the equally distant emperor of Germany rested but lightly on the necks of the counts of Toulouse, who jousted pleasantly with the Saracen and competed in holy zeal with the bishops for the revenue accruing from their Jewish subjects. "Life was gay; manners, fostered by troubadour poetry, were freer, with scant room for bigotry." Christianity sat but lightly upon these men of ancient Roman stock. The Jew shared in the peaceful conditions, the riches and the culture of this, the wealthiest part of France.

And before the crusade against the Albigensian heretics had destroyed that brilliant civilization, before the reign of terror instituted by the crusading bands of *pastoreaux* and peasants, and before the rebellion of the populace against the heavy taxation of Charles VI, Israel had had a breathing space in which to develop its culture and to acquire strength against new wanderings. Soon, as we learn from the manuscripts of the *Minhag Zorfat* (the order of the Franco-Jewish ritual)— veritable firebrands as they were—Jews were to settle in Asti, Fossano and Moncalvo, and here in the friendly plain of Piedmont another phase in their odyssey came to an end.

It is a product of this gay Provence, the *Masseket Purim*, a humorous parody in the talmudic style, that first tells of the peculiar customs unknown to the author of a *Hymn for the Night of Purim*, who had been satisfied a century earlier with lauding indiscriminately the virtues of red, white and green wines. It would appear

that a month before the festival every
Jewish town in south-eastern France was
wont to elect a Purim king and to invest
him with such authority over the lives
and possessions of his subjects as became
an emperor of "the vineyard of the community." The ceremony of election was
simple. At a gathering of townsmen in the
house of the presumptive monarch, the
staff of authority was formally handed
from hand to hand till it went the round
of the company. This investiture was
accompanied by humorous speeches which,
though as yet informal, were later to
develop, on the one hand into the Purim
play, and on the other, through the sermon
of the seventeenth century Purim Rabbi,
into the farcical disputation of the masquerade. It was the duty of this king to
place all other kings under solemn oath
to observe the laws laid down by the
prophet Bottle: *Habakbuk* by paronomasia
for *Habbakuk*. His was the right to impose
fines on those who might disobey him and

his the privilege to shower blessings on
those who did his will.

When the Jews of Provence reached
Italy they brought this ceremony with
them. That they had not forgotten it on
their journey we know from a poem by
Daniel ben Samuel of Rossena who flourished between 1492 and 1508. His verses
in honor of a boy who was elected Purim
king have little literary merit and less
elegance, but they prove that the Provençal
custom had reached Italy by the end of
the fifteenth century. The poem runs
somewhat as follows: "Happy is the land
whose ruler is a youth of great ability and
who is powerful to give aid! Better far the
tiny grapes of the small tribe of Ephraim
(an allusion to the boy's name, Eliezer)
than all the vine crop of Abiezer. Every
man of years will laugh over this and say:
'Grant me help, oh my God, for in the
month of Adar Thy peculiar people had
for their king Eliezer!' "

It may be that the Carnival Pope of
Rome gave stimulus to this custom of

electing the Purim king so that he lived
on later as the Purim Rabbi. The seventeenth century *Masseket Purim*, another
humorous tract, still preserves one of his
many sermons. In Germany and in Eastern
Europe he was attired in a special robe
and was wont to entertain the public with
his keen if somewhat coarse wit. Naturally
he poked fun at the heads of the community, marking as his chief butt the
Rosh Yeshibah, the head of the local talmudical college; while his theme was ever
wine.

We know of the early form of the masquerade from two other sources, from
illustrations to Renaissance and post-
Renaissance books, and from rabbinic
controversy. The first pictures of the
accepted Purim entertainers which portray
jesters, actors and marionettes, appear in
the illustrated *haggadot* of the fifteenth
century. They are also to be found both
in the illustrated editions of Esther and in
dissertations on Purim by Gentile scholars.
These representations are especially fre-

quent in those books produced when
copper engravings became fashionable. In
one of the *Megillot*, now in the keeping of
the Bezalel Museum in Jerusalem, there
is a vignette at the end of the scroll which
represents a dance of masked figures
reminiscent of the Italian actors of the
Commedia del Arte. Some of the entertainers resemble the harlequin who carries
a stringed instrument which is partly
mandolin and partly viol.

It is in a letter from Moses Isserles to
Joseph Caro the elder that we learn of
the rabbinic disapproval of the masquerade. The earlier authorities (*posekim*)
had allowed the wearing of masques and
the exchange of dress "in order to promote
happiness generally" (*lesimhah be'alma*),
but Isserles inveighs against this disregard
of the Deuteronomic injunction. He
quotes as the oldest authority for the
carnival in Jewry one Judah Minz who
died in Venice in 1508. The date would
seem to justify our inference that the
masquerade or carnival did not form part

of the Purim celebration in Italian Jewry before their community had been augmented by the refugees from Provence. The unequivocal command in Deuteronomy, chapter 22, verse 5, which was probably directed in the first place against the adoption of heathen customs, had been openly flouted and the displeasure of the pious roused. In the course of time, however, in spite of the condemnation of the Rabbis, the masquerade took on both Jewish garb and Jewish spirit and ceased from being an imitation of a Gentile festivity.

What exactly did the Jews take from the Italian carnival? To answer this question we must consider not only the form which the carnival took in Italy but also its origin. The name itself is probably derived from *carne avallare* (to swallow meat), also known as *carnesciale*, from *carne scialare* (to abound in flesh, or use it unrestrictedly). From the day after Epiphany, the 7th of January, till midnight on Shrove Tuesday, the Italian

cities were scenes of public entertainments,
fairs, races and on some occasions plays.
The celebration was one of unbridled
license. Even the popes who could not
offlcially approve of such immorality had
to condone the carnival because of the
stimulus it gave to trade since it attracted
the country folk from the neighboring
villages. Thus we find the Cardinal Vicar
retiring from the Vatican so as not to be
unduly offended by the prevalent licen-
tiousness, yet at the same time giving the
police of Rome, who were under his authority, special permission for the wearing of
masks in the streets. He names the day
when people might pelt each other with
sham comfits and regulates their exact
size and nature. It was only at a much
later period when the people of Rome
were bent on manifesting their discontent,
that the popes ceased from their public
disapproval. The men of Rome desired to
associate themselves with the rest of
liberated and united Italy in abstaining
from the festivities of a papal entertain-

ment; until at length fearing the loss of their temporal power, the priestly government did all it could to excite the people to their accustomed revelry.

The carnival is undoubtedly pre-Christian. In celebrating their Bacchanalian festivals twice yearly, the Romans were acting on an ancient tradition. The double celebration seems to indicate an early connection between those rites and the two main seasons of winter and summer. The carnival is typical of the pagan midwinter reveling which is remembered in the Lupercalian festival in honor of Pan and Ceres which took place in the month of February, in the medieval celebration known as the Feast of Fools, and also in the carnival which is still observed in the month of February throughout the Rhineland. Much though it might desire it, the Church could not suppress these revels; it could only absorb them into its own ritual by assigning to these pagan customs a meaning connected with its own practices. Thus Pope Gelasius I (d. 496)

strove to supersede the Lupercalia which
the members of his church loved too dearly,
by substituting the festival of the Purifica-
tion of the Blessed Virgin with special
illumination of the altar candles.

We hold that it was from certain peculiarities of the Saturnalia which lived on
in the carnival that the stock of Purim
customs was enlarged. During the Saturnalia which marked the winter solstice,
the schools of Rome were closed, no war
was declared nor battle fought, no punishment was inflicted. Distinctions of rank
were laid aside, slaves reclined at the table
and were waited on by their masters and
the utmost freedom of speech was allowed.
Gambling with dice, at other times illegal,
was now permitted. All classes exchanged
gifts of wax tapers and clay dolls. The
prominence given to candles points to the
custom of making a new fire. This solemn
kindling at the summer solstice (Eve of
St. John) still prevails in many parts of
Europe, notably in Germany. The yule

log is a relic of similar observances at the winter solstice.

For all these usages Purim has parallels. Purim sees the temporary hierarchy of the jester, freedom of speech, the inversion of rank in the synagogue and tacit approval of gambling. It will be remembered that in medieval Frankfort and elsewhere ten candles were burnt in memory of Haman and his sons. This is perhaps ultimately to be connected with the fires of the winter solstice. The clay dolls are still more interesting. In Eastern Europe and in Palestine models of Esther, Haman and Mordecai are made out of sugar and pastry for the children. It is known that the main body of Sephardim reached Palestine about the beginning of the sixteenth century. If they brought this custom from Italy where it had been instituted in the time of Kalonymos ben Kalonymos, which is not an unreasonable supposition, then the shape of the children's Purim sweets may well take its origin in that of the sacrifices of human beings to the infernal god.

There is unfortunately no full account known to the writer of the Purim carnival in sixteenth century Italy. It is inferred that there was a great *se'udah*, that the men masqueraded in women's dress and that miming was acceptable. The development of the Purim entertainer can however be traced with some degree of accuracy from pictures. In Dr. Leusden's collection of these published under the title *Philologus Hebraicomixtus*, the thesis on Esther is illustrated by a picture of Purim entertainers. Kitchen utensils are the chief items of their strange fancy dress. An outstanding example of the eighteenth century *Megillot* is at present in the possession of the Academy of Sciences in Budapest. The illustrations, especially those on the page of benedictions, indicate that the character of the Purim player is by now distinctly Jewish. The authentic masquerade was to see its heyday in the beginning of the nineteenth century. Let us attempt to reconstruct it in its prime.

The little town in Eastern Europe shall be unnamed. Let it suffice to reveal that here the center of all activity is the *Yeshibah* or talmudical seminary whither Reb Mendel's learning has attracted the youth of all the Jewish villages within fifty versts. Every Jewish householder in the town knows the students only too well, since in addition to pecuniary support of the *Yeshibah* he entertains a student to a meal almost every day. Purim is the day of the *bahurim* (students). It is to them that the arrangements for the celebration are invariably entrusted, and for weeks before the festival they have devoted their leisure to planning the order of the masquerade, deciding which characters are to lead the procession and composing the dialogues which will draw roars of laughter from the assembled community. They know exactly what to say about the *shammash* (beadle).

The women folk have prepared against

the festival pounds of *lekach* or honey-cake
with which they will regale every caller.
By the eve of the Fast of Esther all is
prepared and the hush of expectancy is
laid over the town.

Long before daybreak everyone is up.
Slowly the winter sun rises to pierce the
grey leaden clouds and to disperse the
low-lying mist which still holds the earth
in its thrall. Dawn is at first grey and
cold till the sunbeams gild the housetops.
The snow is crisp and crackles underfoot
and icicles of weird and wondrous form
hang everywhere. As soon as the reading
of the *Megillah* is over, all hurry back
from the synagogue to a hasty breakfast
and then to the square where the serious
business of the day is to be transacted.
The square is a hubbub. It is alive with
men in every variety of fancy dress. The
orchestra is assembled there too. The
fiddles and the bass-viol screech in unison.
The cymbals and the drums clash together
and the trumpet blares in a noisome
harmony whose moaning counterpoint is

picked out by the droning of the *dudel-sack* or bag-pipe. In the ever growing din the motley bands who are to form the procession are busily parading themselves, each man giving to his fellow's dress that final touch, that tasteful alteration, which will lend grace to his dress and humor to his masking. Then at length when all are ready, they set off on their round of visits to the men whom they have chosen to honor. Their choice, one fears, is influenced not only by the natural generosity of their clients but also by the ability of the latter to give generously.

The *marshelik* (jester) leads the mendicant crowd to the tune of his fiddle. First comes Noah with a long white beard which reaches down to his knees and an immense red nose a foot and a half long to remind us that he was once indiscreet in his cups. On his head is perched a high hat and in his hand he carries a great whip. He is followed, in the manner of patriarchs, by his family and a collection of the animals who took refuge with him in the ark. The lion who has been chosen for his hideous blood-curdling roar, has a mane of wood shavings. The tiger, true to its feline nature, walks daintily and with mincing steps upright, with whiskers well waxed, not unbecoming in a dragon, and, being a prudent beast, he holds a superabundant tail gracefully over his arm. The raven, whose rolling gait would bring him success as a *shammash* even in Jerusalem, follows dressed in a swallow-tailed morning coat and a white necktie, his nose prolonged into a magnificent beak. The dove is there decked out in feathers which only we know to have been plucked from the *se'udah* goose. A strangely lumbering elephant follows; his legs manifest such widely differing opinions on that all important topic, the *modus ambulandi* of the bianthropoid elephant, that he is in imminent danger of sudden collapse. Behind come the bear, the wolf and the fox, a cock who crows unceasingly, an ox, an ass, a lamb, a hare and last but not least an acrobatic crab. He has taken the fancy of the spectators who crowd to witness the procession.

Joshua and his warriors compose the guard to Noah's family. Joshua wears Nankeen pantaloons and a red coat, and has the sun on one side of him and the moon on the other in vivid interpretation of Joshua, chapter 10, verses 12 and 13.

" . . . and he said in the sight of Israel:
Sun, stand thou still upon Gibeon;
And thou, Moon, in the valley of Aijalon.
And the sun stood still, and the moon stayed,
Until the nation had avenged themselves of
   their enemies."

But the sun has lost his biblical importance. He wears a pair of tight-fitting trousers and his doublet is surmounted by a disc of gilt paper, while the moon has a face of silver foil and the red nose of Saturn's jollity. Seven priests, all in the prescribed short trousers, blow mightily on trombones to recall the miracle which was enacted on the too stubborn walls of Jericho. A company of warriors follows dressed up in jackboots, discarded mili-

tary coats and cocked hats. Their arms
are mighty spears of wood well pasted
over with tin foil. Next come two
bahurim who travesty David and Goliath.
Goliath's head is a very beer-barrel and
David is compensated for his shortness by
his corpulence. Whenever he can he crawls
in between the legs of Goliath and smites
him lustily behind, to the unrestrained
and delighted laughter of the onlookers.
And thus both singly and in groups all the
characters of the Bible story pass on.
They visit house after house, repeating
the songs, the dialogues and the poems
which they prepared for this occasion.
The streets ring again with laughter as
they jest and wander on.

Before Purim the students have, with
the aid of the *Parnasim* (elders) of the
community, drawn up a list of the house-
holders and have estimated how much
wine each should give. Every householder
is bound to supply the quantity imposed
upon him and pressure is brought to bear
till he gives in full measure. In earlier

days the *bahurim* used to stitch into their
caps a small circle called in Yiddish
Krentshen mit Varenkelech, which was not
removed so long as there remained any
wine due to them. The type of song which
they were wont to sing is doggerel. Moritz
Steinschneider gives two verses which he
himself sang when he was a *bahur*.

> O holde Schwester, gib uns Wein
> Und lass die hand uns sehen!
> Dann wollen wir dir prophezeien
> Was kunftig wird geschehen.

> Wer vieles Heu im Stalle hat,
> Dem wird die Kuh nicht mager,
> Und wer eine schöne Schwester hat,
> Bekommt bald einen Schwager.

> O beauteous sister, give us wine
> And show us, pray, thy hand.
> For then to thee we'll show the sign
> Of that which fate has planned.

> If hay's in the stall,
> The cow won't stay thin.
> If a beauty enthrall
> Her brother gets kin.

But the wittiest among the *bahurim* have reserved their energies for the evening entertainment which takes place in the house of the wealthy Reb Gershon. Here the family and friends of the host, as well as the principal members of the community, meet towards evening in the guest chamber where they ensconce themselves in readiness to receive the expected guests.

There is a knock at the door. Five *orhim* (wayfarers) are announced. The host directs that they be shown in with honor and respect. Five men of similar appearance and height enter, all dressed in long robes, caftans, fur coats, with immense *peot* (sidelocks) and beards which sweep the ground with patriarchal dignity. Three times do they bow solemnly to the assembled company, who return their salutation. "Whence might you be coming?" asks the host. "We are the five Rabbis of Jerusalem," they reply. "We have come here to hold a disputation with your learned men." Scarcely have the five wise

men seated themselves ere the sound of
fiddles, flutes and drums is heard and
more distinguished visitors are announced.
No less a personage than King Solomon
enters. He is attired in a dressing gown
of many colors, his paunch well stuffed
with feathers; a substantial sovereign
indeed. His tall crown is made of gold-
colored paper while in his hand he holds a
huge scepter with a bladder tied on to the
end. His nose is a hollowed pumpkin on
which a bird's nest is fastened like a
carbuncle. As might be expected, Solomon
has not forgotten his harem. Some thirty
of his wives trip in ponderously after him
in short white petticoats, trouser legs well
projecting, yellow and red turbans and
fantastic masks. King Solomon seats himself with regal dignity upon a high chair
and his wives minister to him. One
brings him his *chubuk* to smoke, another
a huge tankard of mead, a third holds out
for the occasional delectation of the royal
if anachronistic nose, a snuff box about
the size of a coal scuttle. The remaining

wives group themselves round Solomon in
attitudes which are free rather than
dignified.

Another knock is heard and a third
party of masqueraders enters the room.
This time they represent the local *Bet
Din* or ecclesiastical court. There stands
the Chief Rabbi with his three *dayyanim*
or assistant judges. The Chief Rabbi is
dressed in a drover's coat, jackboots well
armed with spurs, a military cap cocked
rakishly awry, and holds a short-handled
whip which he cracks every now and then
to give point to his words. He enters supported with affection, but small reverence,
upon the arm of the *shabbas shikse*, a
non-Jewish girl who lights the fires and
does similar forbidden tasks in the Jewish
house on the Sabbath day. The three
dayyanim indulge in by-play to show the
spectators that one of them is deaf, the
second dumb and the third blind, any of
which afflictions would disqualify an in-
tending *dayyan* from holding office. The

party of Rabbis takes the seats to which they are shown.

Each one in turn addresses the company and asks a question to which his own reply is calculated to make everyone laugh.

Then the leader of the Jerusalem Rabbis rises, and addressing the company asks: "Who can tell me whether King Solomon loved women more than *cholent?*" (*cholent*, from the Italian *scaldato*, is the food kept warm in the oven for the Sabbath.) As one man the company shouts "Women!" "No," replies the questioner. "He undoubtedly had a preference for *cholent*. He himself says that he inquired into all things and wrote that 'Woman is more bitter than death' (Eccl. 7.26), no doubt because he found her so, but nowhere does he say that *cholent* is bitter."

The sally thrusts home. Then, with a low obeisance to the company, the five wise Rabbis of Jerusalem rise to go. The host accompanies them to the door and hands the leader of the party a substantial gift in acknowledgment of the entertainment which they have afforded him. They retire only for a moment. Presently, garbed in other clothes, they return to dispute with the local *Bet Din*.

In a few moments there is a knock at the door. A visitor is announced. The door opens to admit a man wrapped in a vast green dressing gown, his feet lost in an enormous pair of jackboots, his nose deeply tinged with red, while from his pockets a bottle of *schnapps* projects coyly. He is no less a personage than Moses. He bows low to the assembled company and proceeds to explain his return to this world. He is searching for his Torah which has been hidden away under a heap of explanation, commentary and super-commentary, a heap of Mishna, Gemara, *Posekim* and *Shulhan 'Aruk*. Of all these he had never dreamt on Mount Sinai. He has come back to earth to seek for his five straightforward books; perhaps some member of that learned conclave could tell him what has happened. Having delivered himself of his message, he is happy to take some brandy and some *lekach* and to stand by the side of one of Solomon's wives, whom every now and then he chucks familiarly under the chin.

There is another knock at the door and Elijah enters. What an Elijah! A short wizened old Jew, with a tiny skullcap perched on his head and a huge humped back, stands before the company. His beard of deep red touches the floor. He, in his turn, bows low and proceeds to unbosom his sorrows. "*Rabbotay*, it reached the conclave of heaven that in this town there was to be a colloquy of wise men. Here I stand before you and I know not my name for in the *Habdalah* service you have called me by so many different names that I have forgotten what my real name is. Perhaps someone can inform me?" Elijah ignores the applause, seats himself by the side of Moses and condescends to accept a tankard of mead.

Another knock—and a Jew rushes into the room much bewildered. He wishes to

consult the Chief Rabbi and the *Bet Din*
about an urgent problem. The *goya* whom
his wife employs to help with the house-
work has put a piece of raw meat into a
pot used only for milk dishes. What is
his wife to do? The Chief Rabbi strokes
his beard with that majesty born of constant practice and then scratches his head
while the *dayyanim* nod in pontifical con-
cord. The Chief Rabbi consults the
shabbas shikse by his side and pronounces
his decision. The law laid down by the
Yoreh De'ah is clear. Either his wife must
soak the meat and throw out the servant
or throw out the meat and soak the
servant.

Scarcely has laughter subsided when a
tumult is heard outside. Trumpets blare,
cymbals clash, drums beat and tin pots
clang. The door is burst open without
ceremony and the jesting master of the
revels enters in a somersault which carries
him to the center of the room. He accompanies himself on his violin and sings that
King David is at hand bringing with him

for the entertainment of his host and
friends, Asaph the sweet singer in Israel
and a company of musicians. In a few
moments they arrive.

David comes first, leading the barrel-
headed Goliath in chains. Asaph and his
twelve friends dressed in white night-
gowns tied round the waist and with
skull-caps on their heads follow him.
Behind this group some fifty *bahurim*
grotesquely disguised as peasants, clowns
and country bumpkins tumble in.

The music strikes up. King David and
Goliath advance into the center of the
room and dance the *Kalomjika*. King
Solomon stamps time on the floor, clank-
ing his spurs to encourage his father's
weakness for dancing. The Rabbi cracks
his whip and Elijah yells his approval.
The music grows quicker, the dancers
follow with still wilder antics. The fun
is infectious. Solomon jumps down from
his throne and fixing his nose more firmly
on his face takes a peasant woman by the
waist and begins to dance. Moses ties

his beard into a knot and pairs off with
the *shabbas shikse*. Elijah tucks his trousers
into his boots and catches hold of one
of Solomon's wives. The revelry is fast
and furious. All dance. Then suddenly
with a crash the music ceases.

The masking and the jollity continue
far on into the night till the dawn of
Shushan Purim sees the last revelers
going home to their well earned rest.

The tradition of this revelry which has
just been described is continued today in
Palestine. Tel Aviv, the most important
of the completely Jewish towns in the
world, celebrates Purim with a carnival.
From ten o'clock on the morning of the
day of Purim hundreds of children are
seen dressed up in tasteful fancy clothes,
being taken by their mothers to the children's carnival. One child is dressed as
Mordecai, a small girl leads her brother
who is dressed up like a bear, another is
queen of the flowers and there a group
represents Joseph's dream. Some very
youthful *haluzim* and infantile old men

and women are collecting for the National Fund; and there a group of children carries a horse by its feet to remind everyone of the end of Ahad Ha'am's humorous tale: *To Please Everybody*. The exhibition grounds have been prepared for the children's carnival, where we see them riding on camels gaily decked with carpets and carrying bells which tinkle rhythmically as they sway in desert majesty. Neither is music nor dancing lacking. The band of municipal police plays in a large hall for the countless children who dance the *Hora*. The number of Jewish fathers and mothers who have come to feast their eyes on this happy spectacle is swelled by some Arab women who have come in from Jaffa to gaze unveiled on this unfamiliar exhibition.

In the wide and spacious boulevard Rothschild the Wireless Institute has set two loud speakers from which issues forth during the days of Purim appropriate music. In the evening a chapter of the *Megillah* is heard sung in the traditional manner. Towards noon on the day of Purim one notices that most of the wayfarers are decked in fancy dress. The houses in Allenby Street, Nahalat Benjamin, Herzl Street and all that neighborhood are tricked out with flags and banners. There the crowds throng together in the early afternoon to watch the carnival procession as it moves slowly through the town. From the Tshlenov quarter to Allenby Street, thence to the sea and back through Nahalat Benjamin, the carnival cleaves its way through a sea of boisterous onlookers. The spectacle is indeed a gay one. In front of the offices of the Jewish National Fund in Allenby Street sit the judges who assess the credit due to each of the exhibitors as they pass before them.

In 1928 the choice for Tel Aviv's queen of beauty for the year, who is also queen Esther in the carnival, fell on a Yemenite maiden. Great was the surprise and greater still the rejoicing and the preparations in the Yemenite quarter where the choice was taken to be not only a vindication of importance but also a sure sign of redemption. The Yemenites set about their preparations in a truly Oriental spirit. Motor cars, lorries, carriages, wagons, horses, camels, donkeys and bicycles were all offered and used for their procession. At the head rode a horseman carrying a large blue and white flag on which was written: "And the Lord shall blow on a trumpet and go with the whirlwind of Yemen" (Zech. 9.4). He was followed by a motor car in which sat the Yemenite orchestra who played their folk tunes. Then in glorious fancy dress rode past the great king Ahasuerus attended by his chamberlains, next Mordecai the Jew and then, even including Vaizatha, the characters of the *Megillah*. There followed a guard mounted on camels, horses and donkeys, then cars of Yemenite men and women who danced and sang. From all sides came the shouting "Long live the queen!" "Long live the Yemenites!" "Long live the people of Israel!" The group around queen Esther who, attended by her maidens, nodded majestically in acknowledgment of the enthusiastic greetings to her subjects, is followed by the fire brigade in uniform, each man carrying a small Hebrew flag. A detachment of the *Brit Trumpeldor* marches next to the tune of their band. Posters, letters, pamphlets, samples and Purim presents are cast among the crowd by the various business firms. The procession lingers on till nightfall but the carnival continues in the streets and in the Purim balls after which the streets ring again with the song of the returning multitudes. The light of the full moon reveals a panorama of unique charm.

In ancient Palestine the festivals were known as *haggim*, since as the name itself implies, the Israelites journeyed on these fixed occasions to the sanctuary in Zion. Today in Palestine, Passover sees the pilgrimage to Jerusalem; the Feast of Booths, to En Harod; and Purim, not without reason, to Tel-Aviv.

When the masquerade grew in popular esteem among Italian Jewry, there arose in close connection with it the Purim burlesque, which soon differed from the *Commedia del Arte* both in technique and in tendency. Whereas the *Commedia del Arte* was generally a true mirror of manners, the *Purimspiel* was to become more and more an acrid satire on communal life.

According to Kayserling it was Rabbi Santib (Shem tob) de Corion, a Spanish Rabbi of the fourteenth century, who laid the foundation of dramatic literature in Spain. In his *Danza General de la Mourire*, a title which recalls Dürer's *Totentanz*, there appears a distinctly Jewish character, one Rabbi Carbudo.

In 1587 Solomon Usque and Lazara Gratiano published in Spanish a play called *Esther*, which was however intended for the stage and not particularly for Purim celebrations. It is interesting to note that a satiric poem published in 1598 implies that throughout the sixteenth century in Tannhausen the *Spil von Tab Yaklein mit sein Weib* was performed on

Purim. Pablo de Pine, a marrano, known after his return to Judaism as Joel Jeshurun, wrote a play which was produced on Purim in 1624 in the synagogue at Amsterdam. It is the *Dialogo de los siete montes*, a conversation in Portuguese between Sinai, Zion, Tur, Nebo, Gerizim, Carmel and Seir. In 1699 there was published at Leyden the *Comedia Famosa de Aman y Mordechay*, which is attributed to Antonio Enriquez Gomez.

What has hitherto been accepted as the earliest published Purim play is *Ein Schön Neu Achaschwerosch Spiel*, first printed in 1708 at Frankfort-on-Main in Schudt's *Jüdische Merkwürdigkeiten*. Schudt records that this Purim play was performed by *bahurim* in a house in Frankfort *Zum weissen oder silbernen Rand*, and that it caused such great interest and excitement that two soldiers were employed to keep off the crowd. The humor of the play does not lend itself readily to translation. For instance, Mordecai, represented as father confessor to queen Vashti, comes to administer extreme unction before she is led away by the executioner. "Repeat the confession after me word for word!" he says, and then he recites the blessing which Jacob pronounced on the children of Joseph (Gen. 48.16); but every word is carefully mistranslated in a manner which is often coarse and sometimes funny. Mordecai appears again as a *shadchan* or marriage-broker, when the marriage formula is wittily parodied. Esther's prayer recalls the style of the *Tehinnot*, the prayers of supplication.

The other *Purim Spiel* published in the *Jüdische Merkwürdigkeiten* is associated with the *Spiel von Tab Yaklein mit Sein Weib* and probably equally popular in the sixteenth century. It is the *Mekirat Yosef Spiel* which was first printed by Löb Ginzberg in Frankfort some time before the Ghetto fire in 1711. A second edition was published in 1713.

It has recently been suggested that the *Achaschwerosch Spiel* was modeled on the *Hesther* of the *Englische Comödianten* who visited Germany some time before 1620, the date when their plays were published. It is true that this printed play might have been known to the writers of the earlier Purim plays, but because Herr Pickelhering (the Editor's pseudonym) saw fit to have a clown in Bigthan; because trumpets herald the king's entry; because the play is full of wise saws; one cannot immediately assume an intimate connection. The jester, the trumpets, the proverbs; these are the commonplaces of Elizabethan and contemporary drama. Quite apart from the very widespread popularity of the theme of Esther among the playwrights, a far more likely precedent for the *Achaschwerosch Spiel* is the first *Esther* of Hans Sachs (1536). The Nuremberg shoemaker-poet writes a play which has movement, humor and good morals. It is really a miracle play. Though the Bible story is followed quite closely, there are new characters. A herald enters and introduces the play to the audience by bowing and welcoming them as guests of King Ahasuerus. He makes his exit and returns with the host himself. At the end of three short acts which are filled with rough and hearty humor, whose satire is simple and sincere, the herald takes the stage once more and proceeds to give a summary of the incidents which have been presented and then continues to point the moral. Wives must learn from Vashti's fate the perils they incur when they defy their husbands. Esther is a model of sweetness and gentility, Haman a fearful warning to the wicked and Mordecai the typical God-fearing man, the king of virtue and of justice.

> "Als den wirt uns Gott auch gross machen
> Das uns ehr grün, blu und wachs,
> Das wünschet zu Nürnberg Hans Sachs."

Nor was this play of Hans Sachs the forerunner of the Esther play in Christendom. Some hundred Latin playlets had already been written on the same subject for "clerks." It was an age when the story of Esther seems to have enjoyed its greatest vogue. In England a *Hesther* miracle play, different from the one already mentioned, has in recent years been republished. In Augsburg, in 1565, *Ein Schön Gaistlich Lied*: *Gezogen Aus Den Ersten and Andern Buch Esther* (i. e. Septuagintal text) saw the light. The author informs the public that the poem lends itself equally to reading as to singing, especially to the tune of the *Pastor of Kempten* or *in des Bentzenawers Thon*. Racine used the story of Esther as the theme of a play for the young ladies under the patronage of Mme. de Maintenon of Saint Cyr. But the subject of Esther had already tempted the French poets. Andrew de Rivaudeau in 1566, Piere Mathieu in 1578, Antoine de Montchrestien in 1601, an anonymous writer whose play was printed in 1617, Japien Marfriere (pseudonym of Ville-Toustain) in 1620, and Du Ryer in 1643 had all found this biblical theme attractive. Racine's Esther was used by Pope in collaboration with John Arbuthnot to prepare the libretto of Handel's oratorio which he composed in order that music, howbeit on a sacred subject, could be heard during Lent without offending the Bishop of London. This first of his oratorio's ends with a Hallelujah chorus. Giovanni Battista Borghi, born in Orvieto in 1740, author of nine operas and much church music, composed the score for *Il trionfo di Mardocheo*, which seems to have been performed in Rome in 1774. It may be that this oratorio was the means by which a year later he secured the post of *Kapel-meister* in his native town which he held till his death in 1775. And Karl Dittersdorf (born 1773) whose misfortune was to have lived and been contemporary with and outshadowed by Mozart and Haydn composed an *Esther* and an *Hiob* wherein his not inconsiderable talent is inspired by biblical subjects.

The miracle play, the entertainments of the Jesuit school-boys, the *Schauspiel*, the masque and the echo of Elizabethan dramas stimulated the Jews to the writing of plays for their Purim revels. So well received were these dramatic representations that later they were included in the Hanukkah celebrations, and still later in early nineteenth century London where the standard Yiddish plays were apparently not known, certain non-Jewish traveling companies of actors made a point of visiting Whitechapel on Purim where they were sure of an enthusiastic reception.

It was the eighteenth century which saw the *Purim Spiel* reach its apogee. The *Mekirat Yosef Spiel* was performed in Minsk as late as 1858. The *Akta Esther mit Achaschwerosch* was played by the pupils of Rabbi David Oppenheim in Prague where the text was first printed in 1720 and later reprinted at Amsterdam in 1774. S. L. Rapoport's *Sheerit Yehudah*, printed in Vienna in 1827, is a translation of Racine's *Esther* but may not necessarily have been dedicated to Purim. A late Yiddish play, *Haman der grosse Judenfresser*, published at Breslau in 1862, provoked Lagarde's biased criticism. An account of the *Purim Spiel* would be incomplete without mention of the fact which Schudt records that even in Jewry the Purim play was not always welcomed. The more puritanical of the Rabbis attempted to suppress what was a caricature of contemporary communal life.

This healthy tradition of buffoonery and of poking fun at established custom and authority was never lost to Israel. First the Talmud tells of the *Mishvarta de Purayya*, the leaping at Purim. Next the gaonic age speaks of bonfires and Purim petty larceny. Then from Provence we hear of the rites which attended the election of a Purim king. Then came the Purim play proper. And to this day in Palestine such writers as Avigdor ha-Meiri produce sketches which satirize the Zionist leaders without remorse. In spite of Renan who says that the Jews have no sense of humor, the history of Purim masquerade and plays reveals a deep understanding of laughter in Israel.

CHAPTER V.

"They (the Jews) were to observe theirs (the festival of Purim) in a countrie where they could not but provoke their enimies more powerfull than they themselves by putting them in mind of the slaughter committed by the Jewes upon their countriemen."

GEORGE HAKEWILL.

PURIM AND THE POWDER
TREASON, 1626.

CHAPTER V

PURIM IN HISTORY

The annual celebration of Purim keeps
in memory the happy frustration of
Haman's plot. Were it not for the continued renewal of assaults on Israel, the
festival would doubtless have lapsed into
oblivion soon after its institution. This
is the point which the *Targum Sheni*[66]
stresses in its answer to the question,
"Why did the corpses of Haman and his
sons remain on the gallows all night in
transgression of the law?" The reply of
the haggadist is that the action was sym-
bolic: that the murderers of Israel deserve
to be hoisted on the gallows throughout
eternity. The early date of this haggada
and the deep impression which it made
make it probable that it was this answer
which stimulated and may even have
given rise to public presentations of the
hanging of Haman. At a very early period

an effigy of Haman was held up to ridicule, and then destroyed by fire, a custom which has persisted in Jewish communities in most non-Christian countries up to the present day.

As early as the time of Honorius (395–423) this mode of celebration was regarded by the Christians as mockery of Christ and the Holy Cross.[67] Our chronicler says: "Judaei quodam solenni Aman ad poenae quondam recordationem incendere et sanctae crucis adsimulatam speciem in contemptum Christianae fidei sacrilega mente exurere." This may be freely rendered: "The Jews make a ceremony of burning Haman to record his former punishment and sacrilegiously burn also a copy of the Holy Cross to bring contumely on the Christian faith." It was about the same period that the suggestion gained currency that the Jews crucified a boy at regular intervals in order that they might the more realistically scoff at the crucifixion of Christ. To this rumor may be traced the legend which states

that Haman met his death on the second
day of Passover,[68] since a people accused
of burning Haman as an effigy of Christ
might in this way have recorded the accusation made so unjustly against them.

About the commencement of the fifth
century the Jews are said to have gone
beyond the bounds of behavior of good
citizens.[69]   Haman was strung up on a
gibbet and treated with every indignity.
Meanwhile their Christian fellow subjects
could see in this nothing more than an
insult to their religion and proceeded to
attack the Jews that they might thereby
defend their faith. The peace of the Roman
Empire was disturbed and the authorities
intervened. By a law promulgated under
Theodosius II, the public celebration of
Purim was prohibited. However, in the
far provinces, in Macedonia, Dacia and
Lydia, the burning of the effigy of Haman
continued and gave rise to violent col-
lisions between Jews and Christians. In
many places the synagogues were burned.
When the report of these insurrections

reached Theodosius he, with his usual
uprightness and thoughtfulness, commanded the prefect Philip to execute the
new law more rigorously and yet with the
strictest impartiality.   But in the same
way as his normal policy was just but
not sufficiently rigorous to check insurrection, so now his order that the Jews might
not be insulted nor yet show disrespect
for the Christian religion was of little
avail. His measures were too tolerant to
be effective and not commensurate in
violence with the emotions which the conflicting parties seem to have experienced.
Between Chalcis and Antioch in Syria, at
a place called Inmestar, it is said that
the Jews began to mock the name of Christ
in the streets and that not content with
lesser insults went so far as to erect a
cross on which they fastened a Christian
boy whom they proceeded to whip without mercy. The offenders were punished
but the insult was not wiped out. Some
years later the synagogue at Antioch was
plundered. Though Theodosius ordered

the clergy to make good the losses which the synagogue had sustained, Simon Stylites was engaged as advocate by the clergy and this "Holy Martyr in the air" interceded for his co-religionists with Theodosius so successfully that he was able to have the order of restitution annulled, the prefect recalled and the law ordering that Purim celebrations should cease, thoroughly enforced.

But the public celebrations of Purim did not entirely cease within the Roman empire. In the seventh century an image of Haman, which was taken to be that of Christ, was set up in Rome and, so vouch the reports, the heavens thundered their condemnation of this sacrilege.

Helmhold in his *Chronicle Slavorum* which he wrote at the instigation of Bishop Gerold, makes a reference to the belief current among his fellow Church historians in the twelfth century.[70]   It was held apparently that the Jews made an annual practice of reviling Christ.   He says: "Si quidem Judaeis quaedam est detest-

abilis consuetudo ut implentes mensuram
patrum suorum quovis anno ad contume-
liam salvatoris imaginem ceream crucifi-
gant." This might be rendered "If there
is anything detestable among the Jews
it is their custom annually, in keeping
with their tradition, to crucify a wax
image in mockery of the Savior." The
reference to a wax image makes it obvious
that the cause of disgust was the Purim
celebration, and in this connection it
should be noted that a description of the
images burnt in medieval times in the
synagogue at Frankfort on Main on Purim
refers explicitly to the wax images of
Haman and his sons.[71] Though it was
clear enough that the annual burning of
an effigy of Haman was not connected
with the Crucifixion, the libel that it was
seems to have been used throughout the
Middle Ages to rouse the mob into a state
of frenzy against the Jews. In Germany
alone, the revival of this ancient calumny
was the cause of twenty-one anti-Jewish
outbursts between 1285 and 1712.

In the time of Philip Augustus known as Philip the Fair who is reputed to have been fat, lazy and withal a good diplomat, an event occurred which gave him a pretext to wipe out the Jews of Bray, a townlet in Champagne.[72] In this village a man who happened to be a subject of the King of France had murdered a Jew. The murderer was delivered to the Jews by the reigning Countess Blanche and was hung on Purim in the year 1191. Philip-not really indignant at the treatment meted out to his subject but rather taking the just death of his subject as an unjust incentive to attack the Jews, surrounded them with his troops and offered them a choice between baptism and death. Some preferred baptism, but most met their death either by the hand of their brethren or at the stake; only the children under thirteen were spared. Debts to Jewish creditors were promptly canceled and the impoverished Jews were expelled by the barons from that part of France. But in the south of France a century later, by one of the ironies of fate, the *Hymn for the Night of Purim*[73] mentions that on Purim neither interest nor usury was taken, a statement which is borne out by Kalonymos ben Kalonymos, "the man of Rome."[74]

Legend has it[75] that the story of Esther was, in a way, reenacted in Poland in the reign of Casimir the Great (1310–1370). This *krol kmiotkow* or peasant's king, who was inexorably severe in his attitude to any oppression which he perceived within the borders of Poland, was just and humane in his treatment of the Jews, and by encouraging Jewish industry within his domains made Poland one of the few safe and prosperous domiciles for Jewry. It is related that Estherka was his mistress and tradition has it that his clemency toward Jewry was to some extent due to the intercession of this beautiful Jewess. So romantic a theme inspired Bronikovoki and Bernatovic to write novels of merit and furnished Czynski with a plot for a drama of considerable interest.

To return, however, to the legend:
Casimir, the founder of the Polish Constitution, the patron of learning, the wise
ruler and shrewd diplomat, distrusted the
information which reached him at court,
and in truly medieval fashion was in the
habit of disguising himself and wandering
in the rural districts. It was on one of
these expeditions that he met at Opoczno
one Estherka whose beauty captivated
his senses and whose intelligence inspired
his respect. It should be remembered that
at this period the *Books of Hours* which
were produced were more profuse in illus-
tration than in reading matter and that
reading and writing were "clerical" accom-
plishments; yet according to Rabbi Yom-
Tob Lipman Mülhausen of Cracow, every
Jew and Jewess, even in the humblest
position, knew more than one language.
The contemporary records show Estherka
to have been a woman not only endowed
with native intelligence but also widely
cultured, while as for her beauty Casimir's
actions must speak for themselves.

Casimir wooed Esther with such success
that he persuaded her to come and live
with him in Bocholnika, but later, when
his alliances first with Adelaide of Hesse
and then with Rokiczana of Bohemia were
broken off, Estherka was installed in the
royal palaces of Cracow and Lobsow. Her
two sons Pelka and Niemira were brought
up as Catholics and are the ancestors of
distinguished Polish families. But when
Casimir died as the result of an accident
in 1370, Estherka lost her power. The new
king, Louis of Hungary, ignored the furious
persecution of the Jews which began as
soon as he succeeded to the throne, and
Poland which had fostered Jewish interests
for so long ceased from a tolerance which
had distinguished her from most of the
countries in Europe. How far Estherka
had influenced Casimir in his pro-Jewish
policy it is hard to say. He seems to have
been sufficiently broad-minded to have
favored the Jews without any prompting,
but none the less it is consoling to be able
to record that at one of her peak periods

of prosperity Poland was ruled by an
Emperor of "penetrating genius" and that
he had for wife and counselor a second
Esther.

Nor was Estherka the only Jewess in
Polish history who interceded with those
in authority on behalf of her coreligionists.
Dr. Moses Fischel was chief physician to
Sigismund I, and the physician's wife and
daughter were maids of honor to his wife
the Princess Bona Sforza of Milan. These
women of Cracow, Chava and Esther,
sought and obtained protection for the
Jews. In the middle of this same (the
sixteenth) century, we hear of similar good
work being done by Bienvenida, the wife of
Samuel Abarbanel, at Naples. Bienvenida,
"the noblest woman in Israel," a model
of piety and learning, was the friend and
teacher of Leonora the daughter of Don
Pedro the Viceroy of Naples. Samuel
Abarbanel was, incidentally, minister of
finance to Don Pedro. The emperor
Charles V who, if we are to judge by the
letters written from Yuste in 1558, was

an ardent Catholic, succumbed before the
importunities of the Neapolitan patricians
and agreed to banish the Jews from their
city. At this moment when the Jews, if
they had been banished, would have been
at a loss to discover so congenial an asylum,
Bienvenida, in company with some other
princesses from Naples, interceded with
the Emperor. Perhaps the zealotry of
Charles V had not yet become so intense
as it was to become shortly before he died;
perhaps, as the newly become King Charles
I of Spain, he remembered the outcome of
the explusion of the Jews from that country only half a century before: whatever
the moving factor was, he allowed himself
on this occasion to be prevailed upon and
the Jews were permitted to reside in Naples
unmolested. But five years later Charles
V's clemency had somewhat abated, and
when he commanded the Jews of Naples
to wear the notorious Jew-badge, Bienvenida and Samuel Abarbanel left Naples
and settled in Ferrara. Here their home
became famous as a center of piety and

learning, and if wise men of all creeds were well received under this hospitable roof, it must remain largely, though not entirely, to the credit of Bienvenida, the liberal patron of literature and the arts who, so long as she was able, had staved off indignity for her fellow Jews.

When Samuel Shullam the physician and historian, a man of Spanish descent who lived in Constantinople, published Zacuto's *Yuhasin*[76] (Constantinople 1566), a work on astronomy and mathematics, he could afford to be free with his material since the publication was at the expense of one Esther Kiera. This woman, the "Jewish Chirazza" as she was styled in many diplomatic documents, achieved a position of high importance in the reigns of the Sultans Murad III and Mohammed IV and always, even at the height of her power, she helped her fellow Jews. Though not an Esther, in so far as she never warded off a threat of extermination to Israel, the high position she held, which is attested in a letter to her from Catherine de Medici

(1585), ensured the protection of her people. But this protective influence which she was able to exert over her poor and needy brethren could not ward off the jealousy of her influence and the greed for wealth which dominated the Sultan's bodyguard. And so, in the same way as the wealth of the Barmakid family caused their rise to power and engineered their downfall for the pecuniary benefit of Harun-al-rashid, so Esther Kiera's wealth and business acumen made possible her rise to power and ultimately enriched the state treasury by some five million piasters.

It is quite in keeping with the spirit which sanctioned the institution of a festival like Purim that the Jews of other countries at other times instituted their own Purims to record for a later generation the dangers which had been averted by their forefathers. So numerous are these local and family Purims that an adequate description of all would be irksome for the writer and tedious to the reader; but two of these are so widely known and so important that the stories of their institution will be recorded. First is the "Cairo Purim" which takes us back to the beginning of the sixteenth century.[77]

Selim I broke the power of the Mameluke Sultans and extended his dominion over Egypt, Syria and Palestine. As a nation the Jews seem to have assisted Selim I in his operations. One Solomon del Medras, a celebrated Cabalist, advised him of the best augured moment for attack, while other Jews lent the ambitious *Khalifa* money to further his schemes. Selim responded to this interest by treating the Turkish Jews well and by returning their interest in the shape of public offices in the newly conquered province of *Misr* (Egypt). Abraham de Castro was appointed director of the Egyptian Mint, an office which, if not fraught then with such all-important economic problems as it is to-day, carried, in the wake of civic responsibility, dangers which subsequent history was soon to reveal. Abraham de Castro was loyal both to his synagogue, to which

he gave annually a large sum of money,
and to his home Government in Turkey.
It was in the reign of Sulayman II that
his deputy, the Viceroy of Egypt known
as Ahmad Shaytan, that is Ahmad the
devil, sought to make Egypt independent
of the yoke of the distant sultan. One of
his first measures was to suggest to Abraham that the coinage in future be stamped
with his name and not that of the "sultan"
in Constantinople. It should be remembered that in a moslem country the sov-
ereignty of the emperor is expressed most
publicly in two ways only; first, in the
bidding-prayer (*khutba*) on Fridays where
his name is mentioned as "prince of the
faithful" (*amir-al-mu'minin*); and second
on the coinage. Ahmad's suggestion was
tantamount to treason. When the suggestion became a written order to the Master
of the Mint, Abraham de Castro fled to
Constantinople, taking with him clear
evidence of Ahmad's treachery. Meanwhile the Jews of Cairo were left at the
mercy of Ahmad Shaytan. This wild

despot ordered the Mameluke guards to
plunder the Jews, to imprison them and
threaten them with death if they did not
raise a certain huge sum of money by a
fixed date. But Ahmad's treachery to his
superiors abroad exposed him to treachery
from his inferiors at home. Mohammed Bey
at the head of a party of rebels assaulted
and wounded him as he was coming from
his bath and later the mob, encouraged
by the success which the rebellion had
had in the morning, proceeded to attack
the Viceroy's palace in the afternoon, and
by nightfall Ahmad had been beheaded
and the Jews of Egypt were saved from
extermination. The day on which this
miraculous delivery occurred was the 27th
of Adar, 1524. Such was the gratitude of
Israel for their salvation that they instituted the *furin-al-misrayyin* and had a
special *megillah* written which recorded
the circumstances under which they had
been saved from imminent destruction.

It was very early in the seventeenth
century that the Purim-Vincenz was insti-

tuted.[78] Then as now the general distress
in Germany was directly attributed to
the Jews; and the burghers of the cities in
Germany, in whom the spirit of independence had been fostered as much by
their previous prosperity as by the innate-
ness of their love for liberty, firmly believed
that the misfortune which had been visited
upon them was due to these semi-foreigners
in their midst. The emperor's decree of
protection to his Jewish subjects was
openly flouted. Vincenz Fettmilch, a
baker of Frankfort on the Main, declared
himself to be the "New Haman" and
organized an attack on the very ghetto
which Goethe was to visit a century later
with so much pleasure. In Worms the
Jews were cruelly treated and ordered to
leave their homes. But the elector Frederick, who might have overlooked any
slight civil disturbance, could not countenance this open civil disobedience, and,
summoning together a strong force of
cavalry, infantry and artillery, marched
on Worms and on Frankfort to put down

the insurrection. The riot was soon quelled
and Frederick had the "New Haman"
hung, drawn and quartered. But not only
were the rioters punished for their disobedience by the losses which were inflicted
on them by Frederick's army, they were
also compelled to make good the losses
which they had inflicted on the Jews by
paying them a large indemnity. The
piety of Frankfort Jewry is proverbial.
They instituted a new Purim, the Purim-
Vincenz, and prescribed that, as with the
real Purim, the day before it was to be
observed as a fast day. Thus it has come
about that from the year 1614, the 27th of
Ellul is a day of rejoicing in the Worms
and in the Frankfort community.

It is natural that the dramatic tale of
Esther and Mordecai which was of such
delight to Israel should have awakened
interest in the Gentile world. In the days
when the English divines, like their con-
tinental colleagues, saw in the Holy Scriptures parallels to the political events of
their day, it is noteworthy that George

Hakewill preached a sermon entitled: "The comparison betweene the dayes of Purim and that of the Powder Treason for the better continuance of the memory of it and the stirring up of men's affections to a more zealous observation thereof." George Hakewill, a relative of Sir Thomas Bodley the founder of the Bodleian Library at Oxford, came from Devonshire. He was a man of no little eminence among the Protestant divines of that day. He was, in the view of his contemporaries if not of subsequent generations, a master of English style. Boswell says that Johnson looked to Hakewill's writings as models of English prose and that Johnson himself was not uninfluenced by the Oxford clergyman. A rather conventional portrait of Hakewill hangs to this day in the Hall of Exeter College, Oxford, where he was a member. His sermon is remarkable not only for the length of his sentences but also for his midrashic mode of interpretation. It is a diatribe against the evil machinations of the Romish Catholiques

of whom he was a bitter enemy, having
a little formerly used his influence and his
energy to combat the projected Spanish
marriage of Prince Charles.

He says: "These daies (the like being
scarcely to be found againe in Holy Scrip-
ture) I purpose to compare with our daies
of the Powder plott, together with the
authority, the causes and reasons for the
institution of both, that from thence it
may appeare that the mercy of God was
more cleerely manifested in our deliverance
than in theirs, and that consequently we
have greater cause religiously and with
thankful acknowledgment to observe our
day than they theires. In the opening
thereof I will compare plott with plott,
persons with persons, motive with motive,
assurance with assurance, prevention with
prevention, issue with issue, moneth with
moneth, day with day." The preacher
expounds the remarkable similarity between the two events and builds up a vast
edifice of argument. He goes on: "But
I return to the comparison of our Powder

day with those of Purim kept by the Jews. Theirs had the name of Pur which in the Persian language signifieth a lott, as in Greke it signifieth fire, a name not unfit for our day too. They were to observe theirs in a countrie where they could not but provoke their enemies more powerful than themselves by putting them in mind of the slaughter committed by the Iewes upon their countriemen and kindred upon that day: whereas wee (may God be thanked) observe ours not only without feare and danger but with much comfort and commendation: yea it is written by those who report the present estate of the Iewes that this day is observed among them wheresoever they live."

Hakewill's sermon must have been impressive. His recondite knowledge and somewhat midrashic method of exegesis lend his words a certain content which if not substantial is at least persuasive. He seems to have been acquainted with Buxtorf's or Leon of Modena's work, as he refers to the annual celebration of Purim in terms which were incidentally to be echoed, if not word for word then in sense, by Racine some fifty years later in the preface to his play *Esther*.

A century after, the passage through both Houses of Parliament of the Bill for the naturalization of the Jews, gave rise to considerable rejoicing among Jewry resident in England, and though it did not mark the entire removal of civil disabilities was the first of such Bills.[79] The occasion might almost be termed an English Purim. It was marked by the publication of a pamphlet entitled: *Esther's suit to King Ahasuerus*, which welcomed the Bill and defended Jewry from the malicious allegations and reports which were circulated about them even more at that time than at others. The "apologia" is decorated by an engraving which depicts Haman pointing to the gallows in a Renaissance courtyard; and Esther plump, and rather foolish, expostulating with Ahasuerus who has been clothed by the engraver in a compromise between the oriental

turban and the occidental ermine. The
pamphlet as a whole is a worthy defence
of Jewry who, on an occasion when their
newly won freedom seemed to be in
jeopardy, found a worthy and an effective
defender.

Of all the Purims perhaps the most
bizarre is that observed in the early years
of the nineteenth century by the Christian
Armenians. It is on record that they were
wont annually to chant in their churches
a parody of the book of Esther in which
Yehazkel is Haman, Cazaz Aretun is
Mordecai and his wife is Esther. Yehazkel
was a Jewish banker and governor of
Bagdad whose eminence and whose wealth
brought on the envy and the enmity of
Cazaz Aretun. He contrived to get the
Jewish banker banished to Abdera in Asia
Minor and once there to be put to death.
So pleased was Cazaz Aretun by the
success of his scheme that this new Purim
was instituted and for some years rig-
orously observed.

The Turco-Mussulman sect known as

the *deun meh* (converts), whose dependence
on Jewish tradition, though distorted, is
a little more direct and more accurate
than the dependence of Islamic tradition
in general on Jewish tradition, still keeps
up, in all probability, a festival called
Purim.   In the month of Kislev, they
believe, according to their prophet Nathan,
that the Lord will crown His anointed,
and they give a semblance of concreteness
to this belief by general rejoicing and at
the same time recall their Judaism by
having this festival Purim.

Quite apart from the medieval out-
breaks against the Jews which Purim
seems continuously to have inspired, there
has been in more recent times, formerly
in Russia and now in Germany and the
Balkan States, a recrudescence of anti-
Jewish feeling. The burning of an effigy
of Haman has been long given up in Christian countries so that a bonfire which
might be misinterpreted as ridicule can
no longer set afire the flames of anti-
Semitism. But a review of Jewish history

in general and of Purim in Jewish history
in particular can only leave the student
with a hope that Purim will one day be
observed to mark the wiping out of an
irrational prejudice against Jewry which
while it is painful to one group is at the
same time a disgrace to the other.

CHAPTER VI.

Jewish Literature during the last ten thousand years is marked by a peculiarly pronounced continuity. The sequence possesses coherence in a very high degree so that it is more difficult to understand one particular portion without careful regard to a very wide context than is the case of most occidental literature.

CHAPTER VI

The Stories, Songs and Parodies

No man has quite lost his taste for fairy tales. Before the advent of the novel in the west, and to this day in the market-places of the east, the story teller is the one vendor for whose wares there is a constant demand. The *Thousand and One Nights* attract by their wonders, Lafontaine's *Fables* as much by their style as by the essence of wisdom brewed from the stories of Pilpay, and Cinderella by its happy ending.

Post-biblical Jewish literature is rich in poetic elaboration of the Bible stories. Of these the story told in the book of Esther is eminently typical of Jewish life. It invites amplification both by its brevity and by its association with the bitter lot of Israel.

The strength of the Jew has ever been his passionate devotion to his religion and

to his Bible. In the days of the disputa-
tions which the Talmud records in such
vivid terms, this devotion was symbolized
on the one hand by the halakic, or legal
tendency which centered round religion
and ritual, and on the other by the activ-
ities of the authors of homilies known as
haggadists, who let their fancy roam unfet-
tered on the paths of biblical narrative.[81]
It was for the haggadist that the task of
interweaving new incidents and new characters into the book of Esther proved so
congenial. Thus it came about that even
as early as the second century B.C.E.
when Esther was translated into Greek,
the translator saw fit to add to his tale
those new incidents with which haggadic
tradition had already embellished the
story. Moreover when the Aramaic versions were made, probably in the seventh
and eighth centuries, the translator was
pleased to incorporate into his story not
only popular myths but also whatever he
remembered of the appropriate legends
recounted in the two Talmuds. And still

later the possibilities of midrashic elaboration[82] had such charm for the Jews of Spain, of France and of Persia that they would often recount the old stories in a new setting. It was by a process of this type that the collections of light homilies ultimately reached the proportions of a large midrashic collection termed a *midrash rabba*.

The legends woven into the fabric of the book of Esther attract by their fantasy and satisfy since achievement can in them outrun desire. The surprising nature of these additions can be judged from the fact that we are told that Haman hated the Jews because a Jewess had supplanted Vashti who was his sister; that Memuchan was no less a person than Daniel the prophet; that Hatach, the chamberlain of Ahasuerus, was identical with Memuchan who had advised the king to depose queen Vashti, and that Harbona "who is to be remembered for good" was Elijah the prophet. Even the maiden Esther whom Ahasuerus took to wife was not Esther at all, but an obliging demon who took Esther's shape and form while Esther remained snugly at home with Mordecai,[83] who is either her uncle, her cousin or even her husband.[84] These tales are well worth the re-telling.

Midrash describes queen Esther as both a foundling and an orphan, whose father had died before her birth, and her mother at her birth.[85] She herself was reared in the house of Mordecai. Her original name was Hadassah,[86] the myrtle, but the star worshipers called her Esther (*Istahar*) or Venus,[87] because the sweetness of her character and her beauty were all-surpassing. We are told of her that "As the morning star comes forth at the end of the night to announce the new day, so shone forth Esther to announce the end of the exile."[88] To the Rabbis Esther was one of the four most beautiful women ever created and a woman eternally young. When she married Ahasuerus she was forty years old, some say even seventy-four, which is the total by *gematria*[89] (i. e.

giving each letter its numerical value) of the name Hadassah. In Israel the queen Esther ranks as a prophetess. Her beauty was such that she was a sign of good fortune, much in the same way as Venus is the lucky star. The Rabbis expressed this by saying: "He who sees Esther in a dream can rejoice over a wonderful thing."[90]

After the king had visited his displeasure upon Vashti and had published his famous edict, the eunuchs scoured the country for a new queen. Esther, acting on her own judgment, or as some say, on the advice of Mordecai, hid herself away from the sight of men and remained in complete seclusion for four years until a *bat kol* (voice of God) urged her to go to the king's palace. So famed was her beauty that her absence from the assembly of would-be queens had been the cause of much comment. No sooner has she arrived at the palace of Ahasuerus than a great commotion ensues. Her beauty compels her rivals to adorn her

with fine raiment and costly jewels. But
Esther spurns the usual means to beautify
herself, and Hegai[91] the keeper of the
harem becomes alarmed lest it be thought
that he has neglected his duty. He offers
her the resources of the Persian treasury,
but Esther remains adamant. She refuses
to use either the king's jewelry or his
food, for it must be remembered that
Esther is a faithful Jewess. Esther, who
like the Babylonian goddess Ishtar is
attended by seven maids, leads a modest
life within the king's palace till the time
when Ahasuerus will choose his new consort. At last the great day comes. Esther,
surrounded by a host of Median and
Persian women who set off her beauty, is
presented before the king. The decision is
assured. As the women pass before him
Ahasuerus has been comparing their
charms with those of the beheaded Vashti
whose portrait hangs before him,[93] but
none have beauty that can vie with
Vashti's till Esther comes before him.
Her beauty eclipses that of Vashti, Aha-

suerus removes the portrait of his former consort and Esther is elected to be his queen.

Now Mordecai had told Esther to conceal her birth from Ahasuerus since he wished that no undue favor might thereby accrue to him. When the eager king seeks to find out Esther's origin, she replies that she is of royal descent and by skillful parrying turns the conversation to Vashti and thus succeeds in leaving the king's curiosity unsatisfied.[94] "For surely the name Esther is derived from the root Satar" (to keep secret,) say our Rabbis.[95]

The king's curiosity is not allayed. He consults Mordecai and asks him concerning Esther's forbears. Then he endeavors, in the hope of loosening her tongue, to arouse her jealousy and to inspire her with fear for her safety by once more assembling together all the beautiful maidens of Media and of Persia. He hopes that Esther will think her fate is to be that of Vashti's and in terror will reveal her secret. The ruse is unsuccessful and

Ahasuerus must content himself with ignorance. Meanwhile Mordecai is a constant visitor to Esther to see that she keeps all the precepts of Judaism. To keep the laws Esther continues to be a vegetarian and in every way acquits herself as a true Jewess.[96]

When the crisis came, Mordecai refused to bow before Haman because this wicked man was an astrologer and, among other things, had an image of a false god ostentatiously embroidered on his garment.[97] Mordecai, when he heard of the calamity that had fallen on Israel, made his way to Esther, his clothes rent and with sackcloth and ashes on his head. When she saw Mordecai in the courtyard, Esther in her fright gave birth to a stillborn child.[98] Instead of going herself and to avoid gossip, she sent her maid Hatach to find out what the trouble was. Mordecai told Hatach of his dream. He saw Esther as a little rivulet of water separating two fighting streams. The rivulet grows larger and larger till it floods the earth. Esther knew of this dream which Mordecai had dreamt before. He asks her to pray for her people and to intercede with the king on their behalf.[99]

Though the festival of Passover was at hand and the "Scroll of Fasting" (*Megillat Ta'anit*) forbade a fast in the month of Nisan, Esther was able to overcome her cousin's scruples by adroit question and still more apt counterquestion and a fast was proclaimed for all Jewry. Meanwhile in Heaven Satan had explained before the Lord Almighty the folly and the sinfulness of his people Israel.[100] "Let Israel be destroyed!" said God; "bring me a roll that I may record the decree of destruction!" As these words of ominous portent resounded throughout the seventh vault of heaven, there appeared before the throne of God a woman clad in widow's garments who cast herself down and wept in such great anguish that the ministering angels wept in sympathy. "Lord of the universe!" cried she, who was none other than the Torah (law) which God had

given to Moses on Mount Sinai, "If there
are no Jews, what need of me? What need
of commandments in this world?" When
the sun and the moon heard the decree
they eclipsed their light and hid themselves in a mantle of darkness. Gloom and
deep darkness were on the face of the
heavens and on the face of the earth.
Then Elijah the prophet arose and cried
out to the patriarchs Abraham, Isaac and
Jacob saying: "How long will ye slumber?
How long will ye not give ear to the cry
of your children? Look! The angels that
minister before the Holy One (blessed be
He!), the sun, the moon, the firmament;
yea, the very earth itself are moved and
tremble before this doom which threatens
Israel. What can we do for our children?"
And then Elijah runs to Moses and says
to him: "O faithful shepherd, can you not
help your people in their hour of need?"
Moses asks him: "Is there even one good
man in this generation?" "Yes," answers
Elijah, "His name is Mordecai." "Go
then to him," says Moses, "and let him

assemble his brethren and let them repent of their sin and pray for pardon!" "Alas!" said Elijah, "the decree is already gone forth. It is written and it is sealed." Then Moses asked: "Is it sealed with blood or is it sealed with clay? If it is sealed with blood then nothing can avail against it, but if it is sealed with clay it may yet be averted." "With clay," replied Elijah. "Then go and tell Mordecai!"

When Elijah told Mordecai that the decree had gone forth, he wept and tore his garments and, as has already been related, went to tell his sad tidings to Esther.[101]   Mordecai returned from his woeful mission and announced a day of prayer and of fasting and obliged even the little children to abstain from food so that they wept with loud voices. Their mothers joined in their weeping and their crying and clamor reached even up tc Heaven. There, about the second watch of the night, the Holy One, blessed be He, arose from His throne of justice and sat down on the Mercy Seat and said: "What

cry is this that reaches Me? I hear a
noise as of lambs bleating and young goats
crying out."[102] Then Moses arose before
the Holy One (blessed be He!) and spoke,
saying: "Lord of the universe! this is
neither the bleating of lambs nor the
crying of young goats. It is the cry of
Thine own people, the children of Israel.
For three days and for three nights have
they fasted and have they prayed. Tomorrow their enemy will slaughter them even
as sheep and goats." Then the Holy One
(blessed be He!) took up the clay seal
record of destruction and in His wrath
brake it into pieces and cast them upon
the earth. They fell on the King Ahasuerus and fright and sleeplessness came
over him, for do we not read: "And the
sleep of the king was disturbed?"[103]

Meanwhile Esther, sorely grieved at
the fate of her people, put off her jewels
and rich raiment, loosened her hair and
fell to fasting and praying that she might
be successful in her dangerous errand.
On the third day she attired herself in the

finest garments and, imbued with the Holy Spirit, passed with a serene countenance into the inner court. As court etiquette demanded, two maids accompanied her, on one of whom she leaned while the other carried her train. On her way she passed the idols and feeling the Holy Spirit depart from her, cried out: "My Lord, my Lord, why hast Thou forsaken me?"[104] Then she repented of her former hastiness in calling her enemy a dog and now named him a lion and was able to continue to the king's presence supported by three angels. Ahasuerus tried to avoid her glance when she came before him, but an angel turned his head round forcibly towards her.[105] When Esther saw his burning eyes and flushed face she fainted. Her doom was virtually pronounced. Then the Holy One (blessed be He!) so increased her beauty that Ahasuerus could only look at her and as he gazed, admiration growing more and more intense, an angel lengthened his scepter so that Esther touched it.[106] Her visit now had the king's approval and she invited him, together with Haman, to her banquet.

Ahasuerus himself is much discussed. He is identified with Ahasuerus mentioned in Daniel 9.1, as the father of Darius of Media and referred to in Ezra 4.6; he is one of the three monarchs who ruled over the entire world, the other two being Ahab and Nebuchadnezzar. The *Targum Sheni* adds the fourth in Solomon. Rabbi Gamaliel the Second tells us that Ahasuerus was whimsical and vacillating while Rab and Samuel point out his inefficiency as a ruler.[107]   He is regarded as having been evil from the time he came to the throne because he stopped work on the Second Temple merely on account of a slanderous Samaritan report which had reached him. Of him Abba Goryon relates that he sacrificed his friend to his wife and his wife to his friend, but the reference has been viewed as an overt criticism of the emperor Domitian[108] of whom this was true.   By nature he was a miser who amassed great treasure which it was the purpose of the Holy One (blessed be He!) that Cyrus his successor should give to Israel to help them in the building of the Second Temple.

Instead of his being woken on the fateful night by God casting on him the pieces of His clay-sealed record, another account has it that it was the archangel Michael or Gabriel who cast Ahasuerus down on the ground three hundred and sixty-six times. He then brought before the irate king the company of bakers, butlers and cooks who had prepared the banquet. As soon as the king saw them, he cried out: "You have poisoned me!"[109] "See then," they replied, "if Esther and Haman who ate and drank with you are poisoned!" When Ahasuerus found that they were well, he sent for the book of the Chronicles of the Medes and Persians to help him pass the sleepless night. Thus it came about that he learnt of Mordecai's unrewarded act.

Ahasuerus was the wealthiest king ever

known on this earth.[110] He set up couches
of gold and silver in the main streets of
his capital that he might parade his wealth
before the eyes of the world. His dishes
and his vessels were all of gold and the
pavement of his palace inset with precious
stones and pearls. In the magnificence of
his throne he tried to vie with Solomon.

Then did the wicked Haman plot against
Israel. The Rabbis love to cast ridicule
upon him, to dwell upon his folly and his
villainy. The Persian Jews of the early
middle ages used to have a peculiar tradition concerning his rise to fortune. It is
Al-Beruni in his *Chronology of the Ancient
Nations* who has preserved this legend for
us.[111] "Once", it would appear, "a man
called Haman, a person of no importance,
traveled to Justar in order to undertake
some office. He was prevented from
reaching this town in time and fell
into utter distress. So he took his seat
near the temples and demanded for every
dead body that was to be buried there
three and a half *dirhems*. This went on

till the daughter of King Ahasuerus died. The bearers of her body refused to pay Haman, but he remained obdurate until they had to pay what he asked. Even then he was not content and asked for more and more money till it reached an enormous sum. The king was informed of this and ordered the bearers to pay Haman; then he summoned this man to his presence and said: "Who invested you with such an office?" Haman replied: "And who forbade me to do this?" The king repeated his question and Haman said:— "If I am not forbidden to continue with my work, I shall cease and give it up. And with the greatest pleasure I shall give you so and so many tens of thousand of dinars." The king was astounded by such great wealth and appointed him *Wazir* (minister) over the living, and trusted him with all his affairs and ordered his subjects to obey him . . . "

"When the sinner rules, the people groan—that is the picture of Haman," says the Talmud.[112] The rabbinic stories

concerning Haman are well nigh endless.
His character is held up for vilification
and his wickedness is proverbial. "The
righteous have the projects of their hearts
within their power, but the wicked are in
the power of their own hearts."[113] So too
has the frustration of his plans become
proverbial. We read for instance that
"Haman commanded the extermination
of Israel, not God", and that "God ordered
the salvation of Israel before the entry of
misfortune."[114] Of his destiny it has been
said that "Ruling is often the misfortune
of the ruler—remember Haman!"[115]

Haman is identified with Memuchan
(i. e. prepared for punishment), and was
the last of the seven princes "who saw
the king's face."[116] He is called an Agagite
since he is a direct descendant in the
sixteenth generation from Agag the king
of the Amalekites whom Samuel slew with
his own hands. Naturally the Rabbis tell
many tales of Haman's rise to power and
of his machinations against Israel. Bacher,
a great authority in the world of rabbinic

studies, refers to a most interesting tradition.[117] Among the legends of the Babylonian Talmud which refer to the destruction of Jerusalem we find one according to which Nero, in whose reign the war against the Romans began, was finally converted to Judaism. Among his descendants was one of the greatest lights in Jewry, Rabbi Meir. This legend about the conversion of Nero owes its origin, according to Graetz, to the polemical tendency against a proselytizing Christianity, which took this emperor to be the antichrist. But Bacher discountenances this view and holds that the legend takes its origin in the tendency of tradition to show the triumphant nature of Judaism over its most savage enemies. The haggadist loves to tell how the greatest enemies of Israel either converted themselves to Judaism or left descendants who accepted Judaism and became Jewish *savants*. The precedent for these legendary conversions might well have been that of Naaman, the Syrian general, who warred against Israel but was later converted to Judaism. It is Naaman who in point of fact leads the lists of proselytes or descendants of proselytes given in a *Baraita* of the Babylonian Talmud.[118]   Next comes Nabuzaradan, the general who led the Assyrian hosts against Jerusalem and destroyed it; then Sisera, then Sennacherib and lastly Haman. According to an ancient reading not incorporated into the official text of the Babylonian Talmud, Haman had among his descendants a Babylonian Amora who was apparently a most highly esteemed teacher of children. As the Talmud puts it succinctly: "Of the descendants of Haman some taught children in Bene Berak."

When Haman was poor he sold himself as a slave to Mordecai and became a barber in Kefar Kerazim, but when he rose to fortune he became an astrologer.[119] To find a favorable day for the massacre of the Jews, like all good astrologers he cast lots. First he tried the days of the week.[120] When his lot fell on the first day, its presiding genius flew up to Heaven and presented himself before the throne of God. "Lord of the universe!" he cried out, "Heaven and earth were created on my day. Remember, O Lord, Thy covenant with Thy people Israel." When Haman tested the auspices for the second day, its angel rose before God and supplicated before Him, saying: "On my day were the waters above the earth separated from those below and in the same manner hast Thou separated Israel from among the nations. First let the waters be united and then destroy Thy people Israel." When the third day was chosen, its angel cried out: "Lord of the world! there were created on my day the plants wherewith Israel praise Thee, the fruits which they tithe and offer before Thee, the grain which they leave over for the poor. To what end shall these survive if Israel is doomed to destruction?" The fourth day likewise then rose up before the throne of God and prayed: "Lord of the universe! today the sun and moon were created to mark the festivals and seasons of Israel. Today the stars were made unto whom Thy people are likened. If Thy people perish, may Thy luminaries be for ever extinguished!" Then the fifth day flew before God and cried out: "Lord of the universe! on my day the winged fowl, the birds of the air, the four-footed beasts—all these were created for Thy people to sacrifice. For sin offerings and for peace offerings do they sacrifice them before Thee. If Israel be destroyed, who will make atonement before Thee?" Then rose up the sixth day before God's throne and said: "Lord of the universe! on this day was the first man created. His name hast Thou bestowed upon Thy people: 'Ye, my flock, the flock of my pasture, ye are men.'[121] If these Thou wouldst destroy, then destroy all mankind, and let Satan rule!" When Haman chose the seventh day, the angel of the Sabbath rose before God and exclaimed:—"Lord of the universe! on the seventh day were Thy works completed. The Sabbath day hast Thou

declared to be an everlasting sign between
Thee and the children of Israel. Wouldst
Thou destroy Thy people?—Nay, not so!
First destroy the Sabbath, the token of
Thy eternal covenant with them!"

Nor were the days only unpropitious.
Each month in turn rose up before God
and protested against its choice for the
massacre of Israel.[122] Nisan reminded God
of the Passover, Iyyar spoke of the manna
and the second Passover, Sivan mentioned
Pentecost, Tammuz quoted the siege of
Jerusalem and the calamity already fallen
on Israel, Ab said that it recorded a sufficiency of misfortunes, Ellul pleaded that
in this month the wall of Jerusalem had
been completed. Thus the months showed
one by one the reason why they should
not be chosen. It was only the twelfth
month, Adar, which had no special virtue
of its own, and which was, in Haman's
calculations, propitious.

To make assurance double sure, Haman
turned to the signs of the Zodiac.[123] One
by one they showed themselves only too

favorable to Israel till he reached Pisces when he cried out: "Now shall I be able to swallow them as fish which swallow one another." When he saw that the indications of Pisces coincided with Adar, his rejoicing was doubled and the fateful day was finally chosen.

Though Haman had a host of counselors,[124] one for each day in the year, not one of them was as good as his wife Zeresh. It was she who counseled him to build the gallows for Mordecai as the only means of ensuring his death. "If Mordecai is a Jew," she told her husband, "you must indeed go warily with him. You must work against him in a fashion never before adopted against his people. Thus to bring about his death, if you have him cast into a furnace he may come unscathed as did Hananiah, Mishael and Azariah. If you cast him in a lion's den he may be unhurt as was Daniel. Throw him into prison and like Joseph he may come out to rule. If you boil him in a brass caldron he may, like Manasseh, save

himself by earnest prayer. Again, if you
send him forth to the desert, you must
remember that it was in a desert that his
forefathers increased and multiplied. If
you put out his eyes, remember that Sam-
son though blind brought calamity and
death upon the Philistines. Hang him on
a gallows! It is the only way to kill him.
No Jew so doomed to death has ever
escaped!"[125]

While Zeresh was giving this counsel
to Haman, God had assembled before Him
all the trees of the forest[126] and asked
them, saying: "Which of you will give his
wood to Haman that he may erect a
gallows on which in the end he himself will
hang?"   First the fig-tree answered and
said:—"The Israelites bring the best of
my produce as first fruits to the Temple.
Hosea compares Israel to the first fruit
of the fig-tree.[127] Shall I then thus lower
myself?"   Then the vine raised up its
voice and replied:—"In the Psalms hast
Thou said: 'I have taken unto Myself a
vine out of Egypt.'[128] Shall I now degrade

myself to be so used?" The almond spoke,
saying:—"Of me Solomon said: 'I went
down to the field of almond-trees.' Surely
my wood will not be desecrated by
Haman." The citron said: "At the Feast
of Booths my fruit is plucked by the children of Israel that they may observe the
ceremonies enjoined upon them. Shall I
give my wood?" Then the myrtle made
defence, saying:—"Zechariah likens me
to Israel when he says: 'He stood amid
the myrtles.'[129] Never will my wood be
made into a gallows for Haman." Then
the olive-tree said:—"Israel is likened
unto me also. 'The Lord hath called thy
name a flourishing olive-tree beautified by
its goodly fruit.'[130] How can I give my
wood to be built into gallows for Haman?"

And then the apple-tree refused to
serve for Haman's gallows because of the
verse in the Song of Songs: "Like the
apple-tree among the trees of the forest
so is my beloved among the youths."[131]
The date-palm, the acacia, the hemlock,
the cedar, the palm, the weeping willow

and all the trees of the forest refused to grant their wood to Haman because of their intimate connection with Israel. Then, after a long silence, the thorn-bush raised its voice and offered its wood. "Lord of the universe! barren am I, nor do I produce fruit. My wood shall I give for this wicked Haman to build a gallows for himself. As I am the thorn so likewise is Haman a thorn that would scratch and tear Thy harmless people. Since the fruit becomes the tree, let the thorn hang on the thorn!" And thus it came to pass that the wood for the gallows was taken from the thorn-tree. Haman, in ignorance of the celestial conclave, went into the king's garden and, having chosen therefrom a fine thorn-bush, set it up before his door with great rejoicing and singing. In his mind he said:— "Tomorrow morning at the hour of the reading of the *Shema'*, I shall hang Mordecai." Then he measured himself by the tree to see if it was fully large enough, and as he was doing this, a *bat kol* or heavenly voice proclaimed

to him:—"For thee indeed is this gallows
suited. For thee is it set up. For thee
has it been prepared and destined from
the six days of creation." Nothing
daunted, Haman went on the next morning to the *bet ha-midrash* (house of study)
where he found Mordecai surrounded by
his twenty-two thousand pupils clothed in
sackcloth and with dust and ashes on
their heads. Haman placed chains upon
their necks and set guards over them, saying: "First shall I slay you, then shall I
hang Mordecai." All burst forth into a
loud cry of lamentation, the sound of
which rose up to Heaven. It was the cry
of the pupils which God heard and which
resulted in the sudden change in Haman's
fate.

Of course, when the tables were turned
upon Haman, he did his utmost to avoid
the humiliation of leading Mordecai
through Shushan to proclaim the honor
done to him by Ahasuerus. His pleas did
not avail him. The king forced him to
call upon Mordecai and offer him the

royal garments. But Mordecai would not put them on till he had bathed himself, so Haman was compelled to prepare Mordecai's bath and then to scrub his enemy. Haman, still embittered by this humiliation, impatiently told Mordecai to put on his crown. Then Mordecai remembered that he needed a haircut and Haman was forced to act as his barber. When at length his toilet was complete, Mordecai turned to mount the king's horse but the task was beyond his powers. "I am old and infirm," he said to Haman, "and cannot mount without assistance." Haman tried to coax him but without success. Then in despair Haman stooped down before Mordecai so that he could step up from his neck into the saddle. And thus it was that the imperious Haman by the irony of fate served his enemy in the capacities of barber, bath attendant, groom and public crier. These humiliations were brought upon Haman for his sinfulness and his maligning of the Jews. He had not contented himself with saying,

as is recorded in Esther 3.8, that the
laws of the Jews were different from
those of all people, but continued to
slander them in an atrocious manner. He
said that the Jews were a proud and
effeminate race averse from all labor. They
kept to their own calendar and to their
own feasts with a superior exclusiveness.
On the Sabbath day they sell us nothing
but on Sunday they insult us by seeking
to buy from us. So savage are they that
they circumcise a new-born child on its
eighth day. Such men are dangerous.

Nor is this the only satirical *midrash*.
In the legends which are told, the reference to Christian oppression is clear. The
address which the Persian nobles make to
Ahasuerus concerning the Jews is a most
unusual example of satire.

"May happiness and peace be eternally with your august majesty!" say the
nobles of Shushan. "Let it be known that
Haman, the chief vizier and highest officer
of your realm, has called our attention to
a nation that is scattered among us. They

are a people distinguished not only by an inordinate pride but also by their hatred of all men. Yea, even from their king and from their fatherland do they withhold their allegiance. Let it not be thought that this accusation against them is groundless or malevolent. Haman has himself found proofs of everything he has said against these people in their own sacred writings. Thus in a book they call the Psalms, they say (Ps. 10.16): 'The Lord is King for ever and ever and the *Goyim* shall perish out of his land.' And again (Ps. 149.7): 'To execute vengeance upon the *Goyim* and punishments upon the people.' And now, O King, thy judgment! Can men whose holy book contains these passages and many more like them be faithful subjects or reliable neighbors? By the word *Goyim* they mean us, the Persians, and they pray that we may perish. Their Torah, which they regard as being especially holy, recounts with joy how the good and humane Pharaoh met his untimely end. They say that Pharaoh

was wicked and cruel but this is all base
fabrication, for he loaded them with
favors. Again they exult at the fall of the
pious Amalek, the discomfiture of the
heroic Sihon and Og, and the terror of the
peace-loving Balak. Their book of Joshua
records with unrighteous exultation how
they usurped the heritage of the kings of
Canaan. In Judges they read with malicious joy how by wiles the brave Sisera
met his death and Samuel tells how the
noble Agag was cruelly murdered. From
these evidences your majesty will most
clearly see how deeply imbedded is the
hate which these Jews bear to all the
other nations and that their one desire is
to subdue them beneath their own dominion.

"And now, your majesty, their God is
become aged and impotent, and His might
is humbled. His people are dispersed
but their character remains unchanged.
Though among us they are in exile, they
do not hesitate to mock us and laugh at
our holy faith. Your majesty, arise against

them and smite down these stubborn enemies of our religion—these enemies of humanity!"[132]

Enough legends have been quoted to show that *midrash* was first composed to amuse the simple Jewish mind. The commentary on separate verses is clear if somewhat indirect, and the stories woven into the new episodes are schemed out on plans familiar to all who know their Bible. These, namely, indirect commentary and completely new incidents, constitute the two leading modes of *midrash*.[133] But *midrash* could only take precedence in the world of letters so long as Israel was, from the literary point of view, in a primitive state. Though this technique was popular because it was within the reach of many, it was bound to give way before the advance in the mode of literary expression heralded by the few. Thus *midrash* was preserved and maintained its popularity in the dark ages thanks to the prevailing darkness, but soon lost its status when it was brought into the light of a more advanced culture.

It was under the influence of the Arab poets that Hebrew writers abandoned *midrash* for delicate if sophisticated poetry. It is true that at some time in the eighth century Kalir had written a poem for Purim which was incorporated into the liturgy, but his method of composition was too complex to find adherents except in the Jewish poets of France in the thirteenth century. That Kalir's poem should be an acrostic of the eighteen letters forming his name is neither recondite nor particularly unusual, but to unite this with the eighteen blessings of the '*Amidah*, with the eighteen words in Esther 2.17, the climax of the first part of the story, and with the eighteen words in Esther 8.15, the climax of the second part of the story, is a process too far-fetched and too ingenious to inspire imitators. Kalir might and did succeed in spite of the limitations which he imposed upon himself, but few attempted to follow in his footsteps.

Purim poems begin with the falling off of *midrash* towards the close of the eleventh century. At this period the dominant external influence on the Jews was that of Arab culture which, though foreign to it in form, was germane in essence. The Arab meters were adapted to suit the Hebrew language and the already classic forms of a youthful literature brought new warmth to the embers of the fire of Hebrew letters. The Spanish school of Hebrew poetry flourished and caused the Hebrew language to ring again with the cadences of high poetry. In spite of Moses ibn Ezra's remonstrances,[134] the liturgical verses, at least, were appreciated and the most famous of the *piyyutim*, as these verses are called, were set to music by a nation who gave still further proof of their affection for them by making the tunes to which they were set traditional. If the Hispano-Jewish or Arab-Jewish culture was more inclined to be liberal, the Franco-Jewish culture was more inclined to be conservative. The Spanish Jews kept Judaism alive by re-interpreting their faith in the light of the new knowledge of philosophy, and ushered in a golden period in Hebrew literature by consenting to learn from the Arabs; but some of the French Jews thought Maimonides a heretic, and others that the new-fangled verses in Spain were poor in quality and out of the line of pure tradition. Hence it was that Spain could be the home of Judah Halevi and the Ibn Ezras while France produced Rashi and the Tosafists.

But to return to the specifically Purim literature, the Hebrew poet of Spain has at least one wine poem (*hamriyya*) to the collection of his verse (*diwan*). Of these poems perhaps the earliest is: "When my wine gives out" (*kiklot yeni*) of Solomon ibn Gabirol (1021–1069).[135] It is also one of the most popular of Purim poems.

The *piyyut* recited in the synagogue after the reading of the *Megillah* is ascribed both to the men of the Great Synagogue and also to a certain Solomon.[136] One   of   the   earliest   known   poets, whose works have been incorporated into the liturgy for Purim, is Isaac son of Judah ibn Ghayyath who was born at Lucena in 1038 and died at Cordova in 1089.[137]   Ibn Ghayyath's three poems for Purim are to be found to this day in the Algerian *mahzor*; the first is a *pizmon Concerning the days of Purim*,[138] the second is an acrostic of his name Isaac and is also to be found in the *Mahzor Vitry*, which is evidence of its popularity in France, and the third, in Aramaic, begins: *The day of Purim is our day*.   His vocabulary is simple, his thought clear and his command of language quite beyond expectation. Ibn Ghayyath and Isaac ibn Ezra were teachers of the great poet Moses ibn Ezra (died about 1139).[139]   Though Ibn Ghayyath and al-Fasi (1031–1103) had held angry disputation on points of law, their respective pupils Moses ibn Ezra and Judah Halevi held each other in mutual esteem.[140]   Moses wrote a wine song eminently suitable for Purim and Judah wrote a poem specifically for the festival

which was later to be included in many
liturgies. Thus the "three fathers of song
whose sun rose in the west," Moses, Judah
and Ibn Gabirol, have all seen in Purim a
source of inspiration.[141]

Another versatile but impecunious member of the Ibn Ezra family, Abraham ibn
Ezra (1092–1187), wrote *piyyutim* for
Purim. His verses, which are to be found
in the *Mahzor Vitry*, are incorporated into
certain Italian liturgies. To the same
period, but to the French school of Hebrew
poets, belongs the poem for Purim by an
otherwise unknown writer, Menahem ben
Jekuthiel.[142] Little more is known about
Rabbi Yosifya[143] the Proselyte who wrote
a *piyyut* at this period, commencing:
(*Purim is*) *the day which raised up the
staff of my supporters*. Rabbi Isaac ben
Samuel of Dampierre (about 1170),[144]
Rashi's great grandson, also composed a
piyyut for Purim.

Judah ben Solomon al-Harizi of the
Spanish School, who died about 1230, was
gifted with an equal command of Hebrew

and Arabic. Harizi expressed his admiration for one of the gems of Arabic literature, the *Makamat* of Hariri, first by translating the work into Hebrew, a task which he performed in a masterly manner, and then by writing an imitation of this work straightway in Hebrew. In his imitation of Hariri's *Makamat*, Al-Harizi devotes a chapter to the delights of wine which, though not written specifically for Purim, is none the less a poem for that festival.

The next product of Purim literature is one of the earliest parodies. Some time before 1276, part of the Passover evening service as it was known in the contemporary French ritual was parodied and later revised by one Menahem ben Aaron.[145] As Zunz says: "This parody was probably not intended for liturgical use." It is a collection of captions and maxims urging all good Jews to eat well and to drink plenteously on the night of Purim. The style is bright and the humor fresh.

A better known poet of France, Abraham Bedersi, [146] addressed a poem on Purim to his friend and physician Maistri David de Caslari (i. e. of Castalarium or Caylar in the department of Herault), physician at Narbonne. At this period Narbonne and Carcassonne were the centers of culture in southern France. The poem is no longer extant but the letter which it accompanied is still to be found in a Ms. which once belonged to the family of Bedersi of whom David was very fond. A little later Immanuel ben Solomon (1270–1330) of Rome shocked orthodox Jewry by writing his twenty-seven *Compositions* in the holy tongue.[147] The *Mahberot* show traces of the style but not always of the genius of his friend Dante. His poem for Purim was republished separately in 1778.

The *maarib* to Purim of the 13th century gave that impetus to parody in Provence which caused it to flourish in the fourteenth century. Some time between 1319 and 1322 Kalonymos ben Kalonymos, the "man of Rome," published his famous

Masseket Purim or *Tractate of Purim*[148] in which he uses the talmudic method of exegesis humorously to expound the nature of Purim celebration. Before 1332 Levi ben Gershon (1288–1344), rationalist philosopher, astronomer and mathematician of Orange, Perpignan and Avignon, wrote his *Megillat Setarim*[149] about the same time as the *Sefer ha-Bakbuk* was published.[150] These three works and the *Hymn for the Night of Purim* are important for two reasons: on the one hand they are sources for Purim customs and general information concerning the life of the Jews at this period, and on the other hand they strike out a new line in Hebrew letters. The *Masseket Purim* in its fifth and final version in the seventeenth century and the completely revised Purim prayers of the same period are evidence of their continuous popularity. In all the later versions the parody is broader. By means of talmudic method a number of fantastic laws for Purim, couched in dignified Hebrew, were evolved. Israel Davidson

of New York translates part of the parody
on the first Mishna of Pesahim.

"MISHNA. On the eve of the fourteenth
of Adar, water should be searched and
removed from houses and from courtyards.
All places where water is not usually kept
need not be searched. . . . GEMARA.
Where is the Biblical authority for this
law? It is found in the Scriptures: 'So
shalt thou put the bad away from the
midst of thee (Deut. 13.6), and nothing is
bad but water; for it is written: water is
bad' (II Kings 2.19)"

In the same humorous strain it is
deduced from the Bible that on Purim we
must avoid passing a stream and must
remain indoors if rain should fall. Occa-
sionally the humor becomes grotesque.
"When Rabbi Haman drank wine on
Purim and a drop fell on the ground he
fell on his knees and licked it up dust and
all." "When Rabbi Shakran went to
sleep on the night of Purim, he suspended
a bag of wine over his head from which

the wine dripped through a puncture into his mouth."

About the middle of the seventeenth century there was published in a similar style *The humorous Letter for Purim*, addressed to the mighty in drink, to whom a plea is made for hospitality.[151] Two collections of Purim poems of merit saw the light in this century. In 1619 at Mantua there appeared the *Simhat Purim*,[152] which was reprinted at Amsterdam in 1650; and in the same year Joseph ben Gershon Concio's *Glory of Purim*, a work of no great merit, saw the light.[153] Judah Leon of Modena (1571–1648), in character not unlike Benvenuto Cellini but none the less a staunch defender of the Talmud, parodied for Purim a poem of Ibn Ezra against gamblers.[154] As Leon was an inveterate gambler, he writes on the subject from the heart. Menahem of Lonzano, a biblical scholar and grammarian who died after 1658 in Jerusalem, wrote a poem in honor of Purim calling on his friends to join him in the feast of wine.

An anonymous publication at Venice in
1700 for Purim was so popular that it went
into three editions. The book is in Italian
and Hebrew verse and opens with a
Hebrew invocation: "Come, my brothers,
come, my friends, and take my poems for
your delight! On the night of Purim when
you eat the festival meal in the company
of your friends, sing my songs! The living
God has given us redemption so let the
poor and needy eat at a well laden table!"

During the eighteenth century there
was a glut of Purim books. Perhaps the
most gifted of these writers was Judah
Leb ben Ze'ev of Cracow (1764–1811), a
writer, grammarian and lexicographer who
traveled over Germany in his search for
knowledge.[155] His *Satire for Purim* is a
book of devotion for lovers of wine and
music. In language that vividly recalls
the *piyyutic* style Ben Ze'ev describes the
thrilling incidents in the history of Purim
and the end of the ill-fated Haman. He
depicts in glowing colors the feast of
Purim and neatly turns the Bible phrase

to adorn his description. We venture to render some of his verses which describe the emotions of a drunken man.

My gullet is parched and my palate is burned,
Earth hath not water to quench such a thirst.
My head is wine-sodden, my senses are turned;
Drained all my moisture, my vigour dispersed.

Weak grow my steps, my feet slip and are smitten.
Shorter my paces, my feet trip and are hidden.
The light from my eyes has fled with their feeling.
Then up rise the walls and about me revolve.
And the house with its pillars upon me devolve.
They totter, they shake; they reel and they quake
Till I cry that I've drunk pure rolling and reeling.

Turn ye away! Leave me! I'd sleep,
And find rest and new strength in my bed.
Then when I awake, I'll seek and drink deep
Of the redness that's wine
And the wine that's deep red.

With the revival of Hebrew in the nineteenth century a mass of Purim literature was produced. Poems, short stories, plays, feuilletons were printed separately and also filled the pages of the Jewish journals published in Adar. Many have great

merit. Peretz Abramovitch and Shalom
Ash have been inspired by Purim. The
late David Frishman, for instance, takes
up his pen for Haman against a sea of
calumniation.   Is Haman forsooth an
anti-Semite? He knows nothing about
torturing the Jews. A mere massacre
indeed! Today there are real anti-Semites,
men of power and authority, but Haman
was some minor minister whose rise to
power was as prosaic as it was usual. He
presented the king with an attractive
slave-girl and found himself prime minister.   In a straightforward manner he
attempted to kill the Jews and was unsuccessful. Surely the man lacked subtlety,
and so—David Frishman concludes tri-
umphantly—he was more a friend than
an enemy to Israel. Vashti too is hailed
as the first suffragette, the first martyr in
this noble cause.

For all this later literature the
source of inspiration is the Bible story
elaborated by the *midrashic* comments
upon it. The dependence on these sources

has been such that a marked unity is seen to subsist throughout all that literature which has continued to delight Israel on the feast of Purim ever since that festival was instituted.

NOTES

NOTES TO TEXT

[1] Meg. 20a.

[2] Yer. Meg. 2.73b.

[3] Tos. Meg. 2.5.

[4] 'Er. 13a; Tos. Meg. 2.5.

[5] Mak. 23b.

[6] This was not necessarily universal. cf. A. Marmorstein in *REJ*, LXXXII (1926), pp. 7-9 (Hebrew).

[7] The story is taken directly from the biblical narrative.

[8] Meg. 7a; cf. for different evidence Yer. Meg. 1.70b.

[9] Ber. 15a.

[10] *Moreh Nebuke ha-Zeman.*

[11] The article was commenced in the *Israelitische Letterbode* and continued for some years in the *MGWJ*.

[12] Herod. vii, ix; cf. further Paton, p. 64.

[13] Antiq. xi, p. 184ff.

[14] B. B. 13b.

[15] *Einleitung in die heilige Schrift* (6th ed.), p. 238.

[16] "Der historische Hintergrund des Buches Esther und die Bedeutung des Purimfestes," *Judaica*, 1900, pp. 1-28.

[17] J. D. Michaelis, *Orientalische Bibliothek*, vol. II, p. 36.

[18] Heinrich Graetz, "Der historische Hintergrund und die Abfassung des Buches Esther und der Ursprung des Purimfestes," *MGWJ*, XXXV (1886), pp. 245ff., 473ff., 521ff.

[19] In *Purim*, 1906, and in *Beiträge zur Assyriologie und semitischen Sprachwissenschaft*, vol. VI, Part 2.

[20] See Paton's *Esther*, in the *International Critical Commentary*, 1908.

[21] F. Schwally, *Das Leben nach dem rode*, 1892, pp. 42-45.

[22] See Paton's *Esther*.

[23] *GGA*, 1890, p. 403.

[24] *JRAS*, 1924.

[25] Frazer, *Folk-lore in the Old Testament*.

[26] Paton, op. cit., p. 30.

[27] A. E. Cowley, *Aramaic Papyri of the Fifth Century*.

[28] Dr. Sukenik gave a Schweich memorial lecture on this subject.

[29] The phrase is borrowed from Suetonius on Domitian, p. 12: *qui . . . Judaicam viverent vitam*.

[30] I. Abrahams, *Jewish Life in the Middle Ages*, p. 33.

[31] *Purim*, London, 1883, p. 30.

[32] *Sefer ha-Hasidim*, p. 1106.

[33] The duties are admirably expounded in *Mishnah Megillah*, edited by J. Rabbinowitz, 1931. For the amount to be read see Sec. c of Introduction.

[34] *Abudarham*, ed. Amsterdam, 1726, p. 76.

[35] Rashi did not hold rigorously to the fast. Berliner, *Kaufmann-Gedenkbuch*, p. 270; *REJ*, XIVII, 169; A. Schwarz in Simonsen's *Festschrift*, 1923, *pp.* 188ff.

[36] Concerning the three day Purim our sources of information are certain *responsa*. When the Talmud reached its present form some time during the sixth century C. E., not all the problems had been solved. Discussion continued in the correspondence of the Rabbis, the *Sheelot uteshubot* (questions and answers) or *responsa*, which, while they continue the rabbinic tradition in their mode of argument, are colored by the style of comtemporary Mohammedan Muftis. As with other problems, that succession of letters which argues the three day Purim composes an intricate fugue of dialectic. The first voice is that of Rabbi Ishtori ha-Parhi who announces with a clear diction and a simple faith in his *Kaftor va-Ferah* (ed. Luncz, pp. 141, 142) that:—"When through the loving kindness of Him on high I came to the Holy Land, I heard that in Jerusalem they had read the *Megillah* on the thirteenth and the fifteenth of Adar . . . So I

wrote concerning this to Rabbi Mattithyah—
May his memory be for a blessing!—and he
wrote back to me saying: 'Had I been in Jerusalem and had they read the *Megillah* in my
presence I should have gone out of the synagogue
lest one might say to me, "The fool walketh in
darkness (Eccl. 2.14.)"

The second voice belongs to Rabbi David ben
Zimra, Chief Rabbi of Egypt and Palestine, who
develops a variation introducing a strong personal
note. "You ask me concerning the fifteenth of
Adar which falls on the Sabbath, the *Megillah*
being read on the eve of the Sabbath, whether
the Torah is read with the blessing '. . . Who
wroughtest miracles . . . ' on the eve of the
Sabbath or on the Sabbath itself?" Answer. Our
Rabbi Obadiah (i. e. Rabbi Obadiah of Bertinoro,
traveler and author of the famous Commentary
on the Mishna) writes:—"The *parasha* (section
from the law) *wayyabo* A*malek* (Ex. 17.8) is read
on the fifteenth when this falls on a Saturday
and is followed by the lesson from the Prophets
usual with the *parasha Pekude* (Ex. 31.28) . . .
and one does not say the blessing ' . . . Who
wroughtest miracles . . . '." To me it seems
clear that this blessing is said on the Sabbath.
Rabbi Joseph (i. e. Joseph Caro, author of the
Shulhan 'Aruk) writes in his book *Bet Yosef:*
"I found it written that the custom in Jerusalem

was to gather coins and gifts for the poor and to divide them out on that day and not to say the blessing ' . . . Who wroughtest miracles . . .'. And it surprises me (says Joseph Caro) that they do not say this blessing on Friday since it is on that day that they read the *Megillah*. And I too (R. David ben Zimra) join in his surprise . . . for Rabbi Obadiah of Bertinoro wrote his work in Jerusalem and knew the custom well."

This second voice is at first a little puzzling till one realizes that there are two voices counter-woven within it. R. David ben Zimra and R. Obadiah of Bertinoro hold that the blessing is said on Saturday while Caro is alone in his ruling that it should be said on Friday.

The third voice recalls the spirit of the first. Rabbi Levi ben Habib, one of the chief immi-grants from Salonica to Palestine, writes in pious style. "When in the years 1514-1526 I was in this holy city of Jerusalem—may it speedily be rebuilt in the mercy of Heaven!—I was inter-ested to know the special commandments to be observed therein. Perchance my Rock will deem me worthy to do them as is seemly. And I happened upon the statutes concerning the observance of Purim in Jerusalem when the fifteenth of Adar falls upon a Sabbath. Now this was for me a new thing since this holy city was walled . . . but here . . . doubt fell among us in

the matter of the laws of Purim and we were
compelled to take up argument and to discuss it.
And after much discussing it, the agreement of
the majority of the wise men of this city—may it
be speedily rebuilt and in our day!—was in
accord with my limited knowledge. . . . The
reading of the law is to take place on the Sabbath . . . the blessing ' . . . Who wroughtest
miracles . . . ' is to be said on the Sabbath which
is the fifteenth of Adar and not on the Friday.
Concerning the law of the festival meal, doubt is
expressed. The Jerusalem Talmud gives rise to
the inference that they put it off till Sunday, for
thus it was quoted by Rabbi Isaac Alfasi—may
his memory be for a blessing! that it was fitting
to hold the festival meal on the Sunday. . . .
Furthermore we have heard that the great wise
men who are now to be found in this holy city—
may their portion be in life! are accustomed to
observe the rites of Purim in this manner. The
truth is that the problem is hard to understand
since . . . the Babylonian Talmud differs on this
from the Jerusalem Talmud. . . Nor should one
follow the precept which is given in the Jerusalem
Talmud. The great and learned Rabbi Israel
Ashkenazi (i. e. Rabbi Israel son of Yehiel
Ashkenazi of Padua, of whom it is said that from
his shoulders upward (I Sam. 9.2) he was taller
than all those that study the law in Jerusalem)

brings forward the opinion given in our Talmud (i. e. the Babylonian) which states that the rejoicing is not to be delayed till Sunday. From all of which we may infer that the festival meal is on the Sabbath and that with the festival meal comes the giving of gifts."

But the dissension of Rabbi Levi and Rabbi Israel Ashkenazi and their attempt to refute the statement of the Jerusalem Talmud are directed against an established custom. The argument is itself evidence for a three day Purim.

In a book written by Rabbi Issachar ben Susan, a pupil of Rabbi Levi ben Habib, the last voice of the great fugue of *responsa* is found. The work, appropriately named *Tikkun Issachar*, gives an account of all the customs observed in Palestine in the time of its author. Of these Rabbi Issachar was well informed. He was born in Western Palestine, studied in Jerusalem and passed his mature years holding rabbinic office in Safed.

This last is a development of the one which precedes. It breathes a spirit of piety and trust.

"In this month (Adar) when the fifteenth falls on a Saturday, the matter is simple . . . The reading of the *Megillah* precedes and takes place on Friday. In the laws of Purim the difficulty is raised by Maimonides, among others of the fifteenth being a Saturday . . . The festival meal

is then delayed till after the fifteenth which is a
Sabbath, the reason being . . . the evidence of
the Jerusalem Talmud. The first commentators
had grave doubts concerning this ruling since it
is not seemly to have the festival meal on any
other day beyond that on which the *Megillah*
is read . . . (Rabbi Issachar gives here the views
which the commentators took) . . . I remember
that when I dwelt in Jerusalem the holy city—
may it speedily be rebuilt and re-established and
in our day!—Purim fell there one year on the
Sabbath. All the congregation—may their Rock
and Redeemer guard them!—feasted on Saturday
in accordance with the view of my teacher Rabbi
Levi ben Habib—may his memory be fresh for
ever! He was then a 'man of Jerusalem' (Isa. 5)
and dwelt there some twelve years ago . . . The
giving of gifts to the poor was on the day of
reading, namely on Friday, and the sending of
presents, which could not be done on Saturday,
took place on the day before . . . In my view
those who hold the festival meal on the Sabbath
have to hurry and pray the *minhah* service
immediately after half-past six (which in Palestine is the regular hour of sunset) . . . and hold
the Purim feast after the third meal of the
Sabbath . . . In this year 1552 there stayed with
me here in Safed—may it speedily be rebuilt and
re-established in our day!—two learned men of

Jerusalem—may it speedily be rebuilt and re-established in our day! They told me that in the previous year (i. e. 1551, when there passed away from the number of our great Rabbis, Rabbi Levi ben Habib and Rabbi Israel Ashkenazi who were wont to hold the Purim festival meal on the Sabbath) the fifteenth of Adar fell upon a Sabbath. A strongly marked division of opinion occurred among the wise men of Jerusalem—may their Rock and Redeemer guard them!—concerning the taking out of the Scroll of the Law for the *parasha* of Purim on Friday. Some desired to read it and others objected and in the end the latter prevailed. In the time of my teacher—may his memory be for a blessing! —as I wrote above, I do not remember at all whether they took it out on that year . . . The two wise men of Jerusalem also told me that there had been a division of opinion in the congregation concerning the festival meal; some held it on the day after the Sabbath, others on the Sabbath. Had I been there I should have joined those who celebrated the festival meal on the Sabbath as did my teacher—his memory for a blessing!— . . . A few celebrated it on Friday since that is the day of the reading of the *Megillah;* but these, it seems to me, have little authority for their action . . . "

So ends this web of argument about the three

day Purim. During the last four centuries whenever the fifteenth of Adar fell on a Sabbath discussion of the problem was re-opened. In the end it was the older inhabitants of Jerusalem, whose custom had so surprised Rabbi Joseph Caro, Rabbi Isaac Ashkenazi and Rabbi Levi ben Habib, who were victorious. Their three day Purim was reinstated in Jerusalem and its orthodoxy established by later writers who bring forward the evidence of the Jerusalem Talmud.

An attempt has been made to develop in the reader's mind some conception of how the problem of the three day Purim was viewed by the Rabbis of the fifteenth and sixteenth centuries. The conclusion is left to be inferred.

[37] This information was given by Mose Judaic of Aden; but the custom seems to be fast dying out.

[38] Güdemann, *Geschichte des Erziehungswesens und der Cultur der abendländischen Juden während des Mittelalters und der neueren Zeit*, 1880, 1884, p. 211 and *JQR*, XVI, p. 652.

[39] *Chronology of the Ancient Nations*, translated by C. E. Sachau. Further on these Purim bonfires see *JQR*, new series, vol. I, p. 257; L. Ginzberg, *Geonica*, II. p. 1, 419; I. Davidson, *Parody in Jewish literature; REJ*, vol. LXXXII.

[40] I. Abrahams, *Jewish Life in the Middle Ages*, p. 345.

[41] To be found also in the *Mahzor Vitry*, ed. S. Hurwitz.

[42] The description is drawn chiefly from a *Hosafa* to the journal *Zion*.

[43] *Hosafa*, *Zion*.

[44] *Hosafa*, *Zion*.

[45] *MGWJ*, XLVI-XLVIII.

[46] Meg. 76, and *Abudarham* on *Purim*.

[47] *Sefer Asufot* at Ramsgate; cf. Berliner, *Aus dem Leben . . .* , 1900.

[48] *Orah Hayyim*, 694; and for charity and gifts in general, cf. *MGWJ*, XLVI, 180.

[49] *Kuppa*, B. B. 86, Pea 8.7.

[50] *Tamhoy*, Pea 8.7: "Whoever has enough food for two meals may not have free food from the soup-kitchen."

[51] B. M. 75b.

[52] *REJ*.

[53] *Jewish Chronicle*.

[54] *REJ*. XCI. Doniach and Rappoport, *Le Premier Maarib de Purim*.

[55] I. Davidson, *Parody in Jewish literature;* Vogelstein and Rieger, *Geschichte der Juden in Rom*.

[56] *Jewish Chronicle*.

[57] In Abraham's *piyyut* to be found in the *Mahzor Vitry*, ed. S. Hurwitz.

[58] *REJ*. op. cit.

[59] I. Davidson, *Parody in Jewish Literature*.

[60] *Hosafa, Zion*.

[61] In the small kitchen the housewife prepares even more sweetmeats to regale her household. To make the renowned *baklava* she pounds deftly together sugar, almonds, *hubbulhan* and a little cinnabar. Then she kneads some dough and rolls it out till it is almost transparent. A wafer of dough is lightly cut, dipped into sesame oil, then sprinkled not too lavishly with the mixture and another wafer so treated put on top of it and then another, till a *mille-feuilles* some four inches high is ready. This is sprinkled with oil and sesame seed, cut up into small squares, put in a pan and straight into the oven. When it is almost cooked, melted sugar is poured over it and after a few more moments in the oven it is cooled and ready to be eaten. *Sambusak*, called in Ladino *burekas* (? *burjaca*, pilgrim's leather bag), are small half-moon pouches filled with the same mixture as is used for *baklava*, baked, and covered with icing. *Puralys*, the favourite cake of the children, is made by preparing a network of dough in the shape of a jug supported inside by a hard boiled egg, the whole being crowned by a bird in pastry. For *tishpishti*, also known as *basbuse*, the housewife scalds some meal with water and sesame oil, mixes fine flour with it and spreads out the dough on a baking pen, when it is

cut diagonally into diamond shapes before baking. When the cakes are cooked they are soaked in icing and left to cool. *Lozina*, in Ladino *mazapan* (i. e. *marzipan*), in Arabic *hajji fate*, is made of ground almonds and sugar, brought to the boil, stirred into a dough and left to cool. These are the staple confections to which one must add a vast array of still more complicated pastries. *Kakh*, cakes full of dates and spices, *ma'mul*, *zalavyeh*, which the Babylonian Jews called *zingula*, pancakes, *kinafe*, *kataif*, *ba'abi kadirsi*, *kirabiye*, *bulimas*, *kizadas*, *bugashe* (? *bugace*, small vessel), *pastida* (? *pastilla*) and *shamis* compose a tempting mass of delicate sweetmeats from which all can be satisfied.

[62] The *conflas* has been frequently printed and commented on. See Steinschneider in *MGWJ*, loc. cit.

[63] *Hosafa, Zion* op. cit.

[64] The evidence is collected in *MGWJ*, loc. cit.

[65] *Terumat ha-Deshen*, no. 110, quoted in Berliner, *Aus dem Leben der deutschen Juden im Mittelalter*, 1900.

[66] *Targ. Sheni* to Esth. 9.24.

[67] Ersch and Gruber, *Allgemeine Enzyklopädie*, section ii, vol. XXVII; Selig Cassel's article "Juden (Geschichte)," p. 79.

[68] Meg. 16a. *Esther Rabba* 10; for the sentiment, cf. Ginzberg, *Geonica*, p. 409.

[69] *Purim*, London, 1883, p. 30; Lucien Wolf (?), *REJ*, XLV, p. 46; Basnage de Beauval, *Histoire des Juifs*, 1716.

[70] Ersch and Gruber, loc. cit., p. 79.

[71] Schudt, *Jüdische Merkwürdigkeiten*, II.

[72] Margolis and Marx, *A History of the Jewish People*, p. 369.

[73] Doniach and Rappoport in *REJ*, XCI (1931), p. 29 l. 13 of Hebrew text.

[74] In *Masseket Purim*.

[75] *Purim*, London, 1883, p. 41.

[76] It is the preface of this which gives most of the information about Esther Kiera.

[77] France, *Histoire des Israelites Ottomanes*, p. 48ff.; *JQR*, VIII (1896), pp. 274, 511.

[78] *Dictionary of National Biography* under "Hakewill" and direct reference to his works.

[79] *Esther's Suit to King Ahasuerus in behalf of the Jews*, in a letter to a Member of Parliament, London, 1753.

[80] *REJ*, XXXV, 264.

[81] The classic sources for information on the haggadists are: (i) L. Zunz, *Gottesdienstliche Vorträge* and (ii) Bacher, *Agada der Tannaiten*. Of the accounts in English of the Esther material in the haggadah most worthy of mention is Louis Ginzberg's *The Legends of the Jews*. The sources of haggadic material are the following:

i. Additions to the story in the Septuagint version of Esther.

ii. Babylonian Talmud. Megillah.

iii. Jerusalem Talmud. Megillah.

iv. *Targum Rishon*, about 700 C. E.

v. *Pirke de Rabbi Eliezer*, pp. 49-50, about 700 C. E.

vi. *Targum Sheni*, about 800 C. E.

vii. *Midrash Lekah Tob.*

viii. *Midrash Abba Goryon.*

ix. *Midrash Tehillim* to psalm 22.

x. *Helma de Mordekai.*

xi. *Midrash Megillat Ester.*

xii. *Yalkut Shim'oni* to Esther.

xiii. *Yosippon*, 10th century C. E.

xiv. *Midrash Rabba* to Esther.

[82] By this is meant not necessarily the independent homily but rather that modification or embellishment of the existing *midrash*—a process which of itself indicates the esteem in which *midrash* was held.

[83] *Zohar*, III, 2756–2766.

[84] Meg. 13a.

[85] *Mid. Ps.* 22, p. 192 and Meg. 13a.

[86] *Mid. Rab.* to chapter 1.

[87] Meg. 13.

[88] Yoma 29.

[89] *Esther Rab.* 2.7.

[90] Ber. 57.

[91] *Targ. Sheni* to 2.7.

[92] Meg. 13a.

[93] *Mid. Abba Goryon*, p. 19.

[94] Meg. 13; *Esther Rab.* 2.20.

[95] Meg. 13a.

[96] Meg. 13a.

[97] *Mid. Abba Goryon*, p. 22; *Esth. Rab.* 2. 25.

[98] *Mid. Abba Goryon*, p. 35; Meg. 15a.

[99] *Yos.* 4; *Esther Rab.* 4.7.

[100] *Mid. Abba Goryon*, pp. 32-35.

[101] Cf. Esth. 4.2.

[102] *Mid. Abba Goryon*, pp. 37-38.

[103] Esth. 6.1.

[104] Ps. 22.1; Meg. 15a, b.

[105] *Mid. Ps.* 22, p. 194.

[106] Meg. 15b.

[107] Meg. 12a.

[108] *Mid. Abba Goryon*, 17.2; *Esth. Rab.*, p. 9.

[109] *Mid. Abba Goryon*, pp. 38, 39.

[110] *Esth. Rab.*, pp. 1, 9, 10.

[111] *The Chronology of Ancient Nations . . .* of . . . Alberuni . . . Translated . . . by C. E. Sachau, London, 1879.

[112] Meg. 11.

[113] *Esth. Rab.*, p. 34.

[114] *Esth. Rab.* p. 34.

[115] *Esth. Rab.* p. 50.

[116] Esth. 1.14.

[117] *REJ*, V, 178ff.

[118] Sanh. 96.

[119] Meg. 16a.

[120] *Mid. Abba Goryon*, pp. 24, 25.

[121] Ezek. 34.31.

[122] *Mid. Abba Goryon*, p. 29.

[123] *Mid. Abba Goryon*, p. 26.

[124] *Mid. Abba Goryon*, pp. 36-37.

[125] *Targ. Sheni* to 5.13.

[126] *Mid. Abba Goryon*, pp. 41-42.

[127] Hos. 9.10.

[128] Ps. 80.9.

[129] Zech. 1.8.

[130] Jer. 22.16.

[131] 2.3.

[132] *Targ. Sheni* to 3.8.

[133] This is apparent from the legends quoted.

[134] *Kitab al Muhadarah;* Schreiner in *REJ*, XXI, XXII.

[135] The edition of his poems referred to was that by Bialik and Ravnitzky.

[136] In the *Mahzor Vitry*, published in the *Mekize Nirdamim* series, edited by S. Hurwitz, Berlin, 1889-93.

[137] Cf. Margolis and Marx, *History of the Jewish People*, pp. 322, 326.

[138] From an Aramaic word "to answer", and referring technically to an arrangement in strophes of rhymed verses for liturgical use.

[139] Margolis and Marx, op. cit., 326.

[140] Cf. Margolis and Marx, op. cit., ch. XLVIII.

[141] Op. cit., p. 326.

[142] In *Mahzor Vitry*.

[143] In *Mahzor Vitry*.

[144] In *Mahzor Vitry*.

[145] Cf. C. D. Rappoport and the author in *REJ*, vol. XCI.

[146] Cf. the author in *JQR*, new series, XXII (1932), pp. 63–69.

[147] Margolis and Marx, op. cit., p. 480. In 1778 there was published at Berlin a separate edition of Immanuel's Purim poem entitled *Sefer Mahberet tofet wa'eden, umahberet purim.''*

[148] I. Davidson, *Parody in Jewish Literature*, 1907, pp. 19-29, 115-134.

[149] I. Davidson, op. cit., pp. 23-27, 115-134.

[150] I. Davidson, op. cit., pp. 25, 27.

[151] I. Davidson, op. cit., p. 40.

[152] The same work appeared twice; first in 1619 at Mantua entitled, *Shir naeh bahadurim, lehit'anneg bo ha-ne'arim, lezammer le simhat purim*, and again in 1650 at Amsterdam (?) under the title: *Simhat purim ba'ir ha-bezurah veha-mehulalah glukstadt*.

[153] The book which appeared in 1627 was entitled *Bashamayim rosh le-zammer . . . be-tiferet Purim*.

[154] I. Davidson, op. cit., pp. 148-151.

[155] I. Davidson, op. cit., pp. 55-6, 206-208.

BIBLIOGRAPHY

OF THE WORKS IN EUROPEAN LANGUAGES
MOST FREQUENTLY CONSULTED

1. I. ABRAHAMS, *Jewish Life in the Middle Ages*, London, 1896.
2. A. BERLINER, *Aus dem Leben der deutschen Juden im Mittelalter*, Berlin, 1900.
3. J. C. G. BODENSCHATZ, *Kirchliche Verfassung der heutigen Juden, sonderlich Deren in Deutschland*, Erlangen, 1748.
4. M. BRÜCK, *Pharisäische Volkssitten und Ritualien in ihrer Entstehung und geschichtlichen Entwicklung*, Frankfort on Main, 1840.
5. CALMET, *Dom Augustin Abbot of Senones*. Dictionary of the Holy Bible Translated into English by D'Oyley and Colson, London, 1732.
6. S. CASSEL, in *Ersch and Grüber's Encyclopedia*, section ii, part 27, p. 78.
7. I. Davidson, *Parody in Jewish Literature*, New York, 1907.
8. L. Ginzberg, *The Legends of the Jews*, 1909-28.
9. M. GÜDEMANN, *Geschichte des Erziehungswesens und der Cultur der abendländischen Juden während des Mittelalters und der neueren Zeit*, Vienna, 1880, '84.

10. H. Malter, Article on Purim in the *Jewish Encyclopedia*.
11. Margolis and Marx, *A History of the Jewish People*, 1927.
12. Paton, L. B., *The Book of Esther*, Edinburgh, 1908.
13. "Purim," *A New-fashioned Annual for an Old-fashioned Feast*, London, 1883.
14. Schickard, Wilhelmus the Elder, *Purim, sive Bacchanalia Judaeorum*, Tübingen, 1633.
15. Schudt, *Jüdische Merkwürdigkeiten*, Frankfort on Main, 1714.
16. Steinschneider, M., "Purim und Parodie" in (a) *Israelietische Letterbode* (b) *MGWJ*, XLVI-XLVIII.
17. Vogelstein and Rieger, *Geschichte der Juden in Rom*, 1896.

INDEX

A

ABARBANEL, Bienvenida protectress of Jews, 181–182.

Abba Goryon, on Ahasuerus, 212.

Abudarham, on Purim customs, 69.

Abraham ibn Ezra, wrote *piqut* for Purim, 77, 236.

Aden, observance of fast of Esther, 65; Purim customs, 71, 80, 96.

Aha of Shabha, on fast of Esther, 65.

Ahasuerus, in book of Esther, 10; in Herodotus, 25; in the Esther-nameh, 116; in legends, 201ff., 212.

Ahmad Shaytan and Abraham de Castro, 186.

Akabs, name for Purim, 104.

Arbuthnot John, used Racine's Esther, 164.

Armenians, celebration of Purim, 194.

Augustine, on book of Esther, 27.

Avignon, charity given on Purim, 98.

B

BACHER, WILHELM, quotes Purim legend, 216.

BEDERSI, ABRAHAM, wrote a Purim parody, 238.

Ben Sira, does not mention Book of Esther, 30.

Benjamin the Scribe, describes Purim in thirteenth century, 62; on illuminated manuscripts, 90.

Beruni-al, quotes Purim legend, 37, 214; on Purim customs in Persia, 72.

Bleek, on Book of Esther, 28.

Borghi, Giovanni Battista, wrote oratorio on Mordecai, 165.

Buxtorf, on *Purim Customs*, 70, 192.

C

D

E

K

KALIR, wrote a Purim poem, 232.

Kalonymos ben Kalonymos on Purim customs, 74, 178; on Purim delicacies, 100; wrote a Purim parody, 238.

Kayserling, on the Purimspiel, 159.

Kiera, Esther, protectress of Jews under Sultans, 183.

King, in Purim masquerade, 129.

Krochmal Nachman, on book of Esther, 23.

Kuenen, on date of Purim, 31.

L

LADINO, used in Purim songs, 110.

Lagarde, on Purim, 28, 41; criticized a Purim play, 166.

Langdon, on Persian festivals, 45ff.

Leon of Modena, on Purim customs, 70, 192; wrote Purim parody, 241.

Leusden Johannes, on origin of name Esther, 87.

Levi ben Gershon, Rabbi, wrote Megillat Setarim, 239.

London, Purim festivities in eighteenth century, 59, 101; Purim customs, 71.

Louis of Hungary, King of Poland, 180.

Lysimachus of Jerusalem translated Purim epistle, 48.

M

MACCABEES, second book of, mentions Purim, 30, 51.

Maccabaens, Judas, victory over Nicanor as possible origin of Purim, 33?

Mahzor, Vitry, quotes Yehudai Gaon, 63; contains Purim poems, 235, 236.

Masquerades on Purim, 106, 110, 113, 125ff.; a reconstruction 138ff.; in Tel Aviv 154ff.

Masseket Purim on Provençal Customs, 128.

Megillah, see Esther, book of; and as works of art, 90.